CROSSING
THE LINE

CROSSING THE LINE

Leading to Make A Difference

DR. LARRY LITTLE

CROSSING THE LINE
LEADING TO MAKE A DIFFERENCE

iUniverse books may be ordered through booksellers or by contacting:

iUniverse
1663 Liberty Drive
Bloomington, IN 47403
www.iuniverse.com
844-349-9409

ISBN: 978-1-6632-1376-1 (sc)
ISBN: 978-1-6632-1377-8 (hc)
ISBN: 978-1-6632-1375-4 (e)

Library of Congress Control Number: 2021901356

Print information available on the last page.

iUniverse rev. date: 02/04/2026

It is my hope that this little book will serve as an encouragement as you lead and serve those in your life. May you find inspiration and determination in these pages to lead above and below the line. Thank you for investing the time to read this book, but I challenge you to do more. Choose to start Crossing the Line in your leadership and life and you will make a difference!

- Dr. Larry Little

CONTENTS

Introduction ix

Chapter 1   What You Need to Know 1
Chapter 2   Crossing From Above To Below The Line 11
Chapter 3   Crossing From Below To Above The Line 18
Chapter 4   Breaking It Down 24
Chapter 5   The Monster 41
Chapter 6   Aligning the Process 58
Chapter 7   EQ or IQ? 73
Chapter 8   You Gotta Have It: GRIT 80

Conclusion 101
Acknowledgements 107

INTRODUCTION

An elderly woman stood before a judge in a courtroom. She had been caught shoplifting a can of peaches from the grocery store and was awaiting sentencing.

In the back of the courtroom sat an older gentleman, who was the woman's husband. Just before the judge passed down his sentence, the old woman looked back, and saw her loyal husband sitting quietly, waiting to implore the judge for leniency on her behalf.

The judge said to her, "You have been caught shoplifting a can of peaches. My rule is that for every item stolen, you get one month in jail. Your can of peaches had three peaches in it, so I am going to sentence you to three months in jail."

After the judge finished speaking, the woman's husband raised his hand and said:

"Your honor—she stole a can of peas too!"

So often, we think we are on the same page with those in our lives, but the truth is that much of the time, we are not. This is true in both our personal and professional lives. The purpose of this book is to help create clarity in those relationships. Specifically, you will learn to speak the language that connects you with those who are different from a personality perspective. The book you are holding was written to challenge your assumptions and encourage you to lead differently. When applied consistently, the concepts and principles in these pages will make you a stronger, more effective leader, both professionally and personally. I've seen it work in my life and the lives of leaders that I work with around the world.

I realize that the word "leadership" has become a bit of a buzzword in our vernacular, and its definition can feel ambiguous. If you asked ten people to define leadership, you would get ten different answers. We all have an idea of what we believe leadership to be; however, our ideas about leadership are diverse, and contingent on our own experiences, education, and environment.

I have studied leadership for over 25 years. I have walked with leaders from across the world, from experienced C-suite executives to those just entering the work force. I have witnessed incredibly effective, empowering leadership and absolutely terrible, destructive leadership. I have led numerous national and international seminars and conferences and delivered my fair share of keynote speeches on the topic of leadership.

None of these things qualify me to write this book.

I know what it is like to struggle as an entrepreneur. I understand the load of responsibility of taking care of our employees and treating them like family. I have experienced failure. I know what it is like to make a bad decision, and then to have to own the consequences of that bad call. I am a father, husband, son, friend, confidant, and partner to those I love. I am constantly trying to lead myself well and influence those in my personal and professional life. I understand hard work. I know that the secret to success is to pull people around you who are better at what they do than you are. I practice that principle regularly. It is not because of me, but because of our incredible team that Eagle Center For Leadership continues to grow its global footprint and earn the right to walk with leaders at every level around the world.

I am qualified to offer you this book because I am like you. I strive and I struggle and I work and I blow it and I work some more. Once in a while I get it right, and it is cool to realize that I am growing. I am flawed, and I make no claim to have all the answers. I understand what it means to fight and struggle to lead well. The wisdom found in this book comes from real life experience and a desire to meet the needs of people who are also striving to lead well every day.

This is what qualifies me to write this book and offer you my experiences.

This book was written for the person who, like all of us, is struggling to be the best they can be. It is for the woman who is struggling to lead her team with excellence and to meet her bosses' expectations. It is for the man whose marriage is struggling as he tries to reconnect with the one he loves. It is for professional leaders at all levels who want to be effective and have a positive impact on others. It is for teams in the business world who want to work together and accomplish more than what any one individual can achieve. It is for those of us who want to get this life, leadership and relationship thing right. Really, it's for all of us.

I believe that everyone is a leader and the first person you lead is yourself. The question is not, *"Are* you a leader?" but rather, *"How* are you leading yourself and those around you?"

Crossing the Line provides you with practical, relevant concepts and tools aimed at helping you to become a stronger and more effective leader, both professionally *and* personally–at work, *and* at home. After you read this book, if you feel that you have only benefited from its content as a professional, then I have failed. However, if you find value for your personal relationships, your ability to lead yourself well, *and* your professional role as a leader, then I have accomplished the intent of the Crossing The Line project. You see, leadership is not a compartmentalized skill. You can't be a good leader at work if you're a poor leader at home.

Pay attention to the sections of the book that are aimed specifically at your personal relationships. Throughout the book, I will use the term "relationship partner" to describe anyone with whom you have a personal relationship. This could be a spouse or significant other, but it can also be anyone in your circle of family and friends whom you love and care about.

What you're about to read was developed from my experience with people from across the world and in all walks of life. I have attempted to present the material in this book in a simple yet effective manner. You won't find sophisticated, philosophical jargon or technical, hard to understand language. I hope that you will feel as if we are simply having a conversation.

So, what's in store for you as you read Crossing The Line?

- At my business, Eagle Center for Leadership, we define effective leadership as an ability to influence relationships *above and below the line.* I'm going to define what I mean by "above and below the line", and how learning to *cross the line* will lead to success in your relationships both professionally and personally.
- We will create an awareness of your own personal leadership style, and identify where and how you are most comfortable, and uncomfortable in your leadership.
- I'm going to offer you a defense against attacks from the "monster" that keeps us from leading well and having healthy, strong relationships. The solutions may surprise you.
- You're going to be challenged to process through a strategy that is thought-provoking, relevant and practical. It is quite likely that you have never approached your life and leadership from this perspective.
- Do you have GRIT? In the south, grits bring to mind that grainy white mash that Southerners love to eat for breakfast. That is not the kind of grit to which I am referring. Having GRIT means that you Get Over Yourself, Run To The Hard Things, Inspire Others, and Take Time. GRIT is essential if you want to lead successfully throughout the good and bad times of your life. We will take a look at what it means to live your life and infuse your leadership with grit.
- We will explore the most important decision a leader can make. We will also meet a few leaders and lifelong learners who show us what it means to lead themselves and others well. Finally, you will meet a war hero who truly makes a difference.

Taking The Little Profile

Before you begin, I want you to take a very short, quick assessment which will set the framework for this book. This assessment is not a scientific test, but it has been used literally across the world with tens of thousands of people. It is as accurate as you are honest.

If you have already taken The Little Profile personality assessment, you can skip this paragraph. If you have not taken it, stop reading and take a moment to go to our website on your phone or computer:

thelittleprofile.com

From here, you'll be taken through The Little Profile personality assessment. Once you receive your results you will be ready to continue with the rest of the book.

The Little Profile personality assessment will be discussed throughout the book. For now, just remember which animal personality type for which you got the highest score. This is not a book about knowing and dissecting all the details of your personality, however, a basic understanding of how different personalities tend to lead will be important as we move through the key concepts of successful leadership.

You want to make a difference. The concepts, tips and processes in this book have proven to be successful in helping leaders like you create healthy and satisfying personal relationships, as well as to develop strong professional leadership skills. This book will challenge you to learn to lead in ways that will greatly increase your influence and scope as a leader. Read with a mindset that desires to learn and grow. I hope that it will be the beginning of a lifelong practice that will encourage you to grow as a leader, a partner, a friend, and a person.

Let's begin.

CHAPTER 1

What You Need to Know

In order to understand the concept of *crossing the line* we must start at the beginning. Let's take a quick review of The Little Profile personality assessment. This will give us a better understanding of what I mean when I say "above the line".

The Problem with Personality Assessments

After a few centuries of research and collected data, most psychologists agree with Carl Jung's theory that there are basically four main personality functions and two major attitudes. The complexity of personality assessments occurs when we combine those four basic personality functions with the two attitudes. This is generally followed with a plethora of details about each combination. (Introduction to Psychology —Psychodynamic Theories by Michael Paskas) There are numerous assessment tools that provide this kind of data. While many of these tools give us a more in-depth understanding of our own personalities, the results are not often practically applicable or easy to use on a daily basis.

At some point, you may have taken one of these comprehensive psychological evaluations or personality assessments and received tons of information about yourself that was generally accurate and insightful, but more than likely it wasn't delivered in a way that you could easily remember, much less practically apply all of that information in your day-to-day life or in your interactions with other people. This is the problem with many comprehensive psychological evaluation tools; all the information is intriguing, interesting and maybe even eye-opening. However, at the end of the day, it's not practical to use this information in our personal lives or in our professional lives.

I say that it is not practical because to me, practical is defined as something that is easily used, easily retained and can be easily applied in every-day circumstances. I've found that, in general, most people don't have the time or energy to take a deep dive into learning about the nuances and application of their own psychological profile, and they especially don't have the time to learn about the ins and outs of the personalities of others. What most people that I encounter really want is the ability to understand themselves and understand others in a way that will practically help them to succeed in their relationships on both a professional and a personal level. After all, people are people, whether they're at home or in the workplace. This desire for a practical personality tool is what led me to develop The Little Profile personality assessment and write the *Make A Difference* book.

Reviewing The Little Profile Personalities

Let's take a look at the four basic types of personality that I use in The Little Profile personality assessment.

People-Loving Parrots

First, there is the People-Loving Parrot. This is a personality that loves people. They love to laugh, they love to tell stories, and they are very verbal. This personality is generally extroverted and is comfortable in groups. They love social settings and love to connect with others. People-Loving Parrots have a wonderful skill of truly caring about and understanding people. They have the natural ability to read others' feelings with accuracy. They are natural connectors and thus can be powerful influencers.

However, People-Loving Parrots can wear their feelings on their sleeves. They are sensitive creatures, and they can be hurt with insensitive words or behavior. They can react with emotion instead of with a thought through response. Parrots must remember not to allow their emotions to drive their behavior.

What People-Loving Parrots need are the approval and affirmation of others. That is accomplished through the words you use, appropriate physical touch and nonverbal connection (think facial expressions). They need humor and connection.

Leading Lions

The second type of personality is what I call the Leading Lion. The Lion is the classic, type A person who loves to "task"—they are a do-er. The Lion has the ability to tackle large and difficult projects with fearless confidence. You will often find Lions tackling one project after another, without taking a break or stopping for input from others. They are the preeminent taskmasters. The Lion has excellent vision casting and can see what can be accomplished while others may struggle to see that potential. Lions are hard workers and love a challenge. They think in big-picture terms and are not afraid to go after big ideas and opportunities.

However, Lions may sacrifice relationships in order to complete a task. Many times, they do not turn on the filter between their mind and their mouth. They can be rude, overbearing and hard to be around. Their actions do not always represent their hearts. Lions must remember that "conquering the hill at all costs" may inadvertently damage or destroy important relationships in their lives.

What Lions need is to accomplish a big challenge or task. That is done by empowering the Lion and making sure that you do not micro-manage them. They need direct language and honest feedback.

Competent Camels

The next personality that we will discuss is called the Competent Camel. While the Lion is concerned with completing big tasks, the Camel is more focused on the details, and on *how* the project is completed. They prefer to focus on the smaller tasks and on creating and working within processes and systems, and they generally have a logical, processing, analytical mindset. They want to follow the steps and the rules that have been laid out, and they will ensure that every "i" is dotted and every "t" is crossed. These are the people that read the entire instruction manual for the new microwave in the break room cover to cover, and then file it away in an alphabetized, color-coded filing cabinet for future reference. They are the go-to people when you need a job accomplished with excellence and precision.

However, the Camel can become critical of others and can be seen as negative and irritating. Their logical approach to life can come across as prickly with a lack of ability to connect with those around them. Camels must remember that no one can meet their perfectionistic expectations and they must not allow this to damage important relationships.

What Camels need is clarity gained through processes and procedures. This can be accomplished by giving specific details and by listening to their details. They need to be validated for their competency and quality.

Tranquil Turtles

The final personality that we will discuss is the Tranquil Turtle. The Tranquil Turtle is not people-oriented like a People-Loving Parrot, but rather they are *person*-oriented. Turtles tend to be driven by a few significant relationships. Turtles flourish when they are in purposeful and meaningful one-on-one conversations; they like to go deep. Trust is vital to the success of any relationship developed with Turtles. Consequently, the Turtle can teach us much about that important trait of trust, which we will discuss later in this book. The Turtle possesses wisdom and is an intuitive thinker. While the Turtle may not use very many words, when they do speak, you should listen. The Turtle has a keen insight and the ability to make strong effective decisions, especially during a crisis. Generally, they do not panic.

However, Turtles need time to process and think before making major decisions, or for that matter, any decision at all. They can easily fall into the trap of procrastination and stagnation. This can cause confusion, lack of clarity or direction and frustration from those in their lives. Turtles must remember that not making a decision is making a decision. Polarizing with no action can cause relationships to struggle resulting in a decrease of trust.

What Turtles need is investment in the relationships that are important to them. In other words, if you care about the Turtle, you care about the small circle of important relationships in their life. This can be achieved in only one way: TIME. Take the time to listen and allow the Turtle the time and space to speak. The investment will pay high dividends.

Why We Use Word Pictures

If you are new to the Make A Difference concepts, you may be surprised that I "label" each personality type using animal names. At first glance, these names might seem silly and trite, and you may believe that they don't belong in a professional personality tool to be used in the workplace. Let me take a moment to explain to you why I did that.

White picket fence.

As you read this book, right now you are thinking of a white picket fence. You may say that you are choosing not to think of a white picket fence but in actuality that is exactly what you are doing—you can see that white picket fence in your mind's eye right now. Your brain can process a word picture much faster than a generic number, color, or letter that is unassigned to a visual. Because I want to provide you with a tool that is practical, simple, and effective, I've chosen to use animal word pictures to help us quickly recall and understand different types of personalities. By the way, these Make A Difference word pictures have been taught and effectively used across the world in different countries and cultures. I've been using them for over 20 years now, because they work.

The Personality Diagram

Now that I have given you a brief overview of the four personalities and an explanation for why we use the animal names to create word pictures, let's break it down into an even simpler format. Take a look at this diagram.

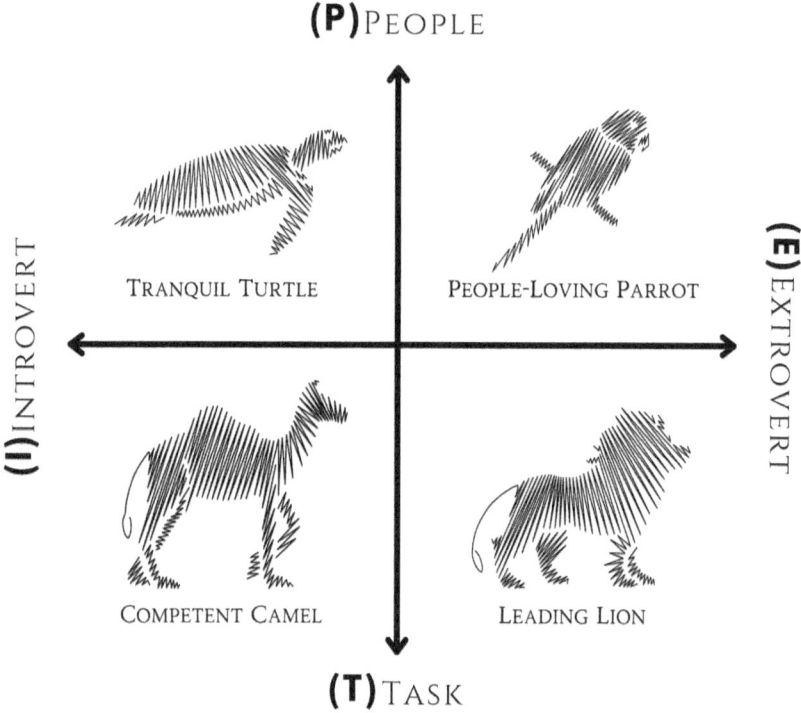

The Make A Difference DNA Diagram

This represents two continuums. The horizontal line represents the spectrum of personalities that lie between being *extroverted* and *introverted*. The vertical line represents the spectrum of motivation, from *people* to *tasks*.

For example, in the top right quadrant you will see the People-Loving Parrot. Generally, Parrots are extroverted, and people oriented. However, be aware that any personality can fall anywhere within the quadrant. This is a measurement of where your personality tends to fall within spectrums, not where you belong in one of four extremes. In other words, some Parrots may be more people-oriented and less extroverted while others may be more extroverted and less people-oriented.

Let me remind you that this system is not meant to label the entirety of any human's complex personality make-up. The truth is that we are all a combination of each of these personality types. That is what makes up the complexity of our life and our relationships. People can and will change personalities and move to a different quadrant depending upon the environment and the situation that is at hand. A Parrot at home may be a Lion at work, and a Turtle on vacation may slide into Camel mode in a time of crisis.

Looking back to the quadrant, you can see that our People-Loving Parrots are people-oriented extroverts, while the Leading Lion is a task-oriented extrovert. The Competent Camel is an introvert that is task-oriented, and our Tranquil Turtles are *person*-oriented introverts.

Based on this diagram, it would be safe to say that Parrots and Turtles most naturally operate above the horizontal line in the diagram—they are people (or person) driven, or *people-oriented*. It would also be correct to assume that Lions and Camels generally operate below the horizontal line—they are driven by tasks, or *task-oriented*.

Personality Does Not Equal Behavior

Now before you take that thought process to the extreme and think that only Parrots and Turtles can be "above the line" leaders, remember this very important concept: **Your personality type does not mandate how you should lead or behave at all times.** Your personality type gives insight into your tendencies and predispositions, and into how you will operate most comfortably—*but leadership is not about being comfortable.* Leadership is about understanding who you are, who those around you are, and choosing to move from quadrant to quadrant as needed to accomplish a goal, execute a task with excellence, inspire a team, or grow a relationship.

We all move between each of these four quadrants throughout our lives and even throughout our day, depending on the environment and situation in which we find ourselves. Many of us move between quadrants unknowingly and without much thought, deferring to our natural tendencies and habits, and spending the most time in the quadrant where we are most comfortable. The key to using the Make A Difference tool successfully is the realization that we must intentionally choose which quadrant we need to be operating out of, in the context of a given moment, task, situation, or relationship. Understanding your own personality tendencies and those of the people around you is only half the battle—the real benefit comes in understanding the entire diagram, and being able to move between each quadrant as you navigate situations and relationships.

Quadrant Map

Given the truth that we must choose to move out of our own quadrant and into another based on the context, we need to understand which quadrant to "move into" and operate from in a given situation. This can be challenging and requires practice to consistently get it right. We're going to spend a good part of this book building your skillset to understand when and how to lead from the best quadrant for any given situation.

While the execution of tasks, such as process-creation, project management, and analysis, occur "below the line", the leadership of people, including meetings, people management, and culture building occur "above the line". There are times we need to execute and get the job done, and thus we move into the lower part of the diagram, into being task oriented. There are other times when we need to set a vision and expectations, and to inspire those around us; this is done from the upper part of the diagram, where you're more focused on the people. The problem is that we as leaders generally do not recognize when we need to move into a different quadrant, and we don't know how to lead from the other quadrants, thus we stay where we are most comfortable.

Examples of Extreme Above and Below the Line Leaders

For example, if I am more comfortable operating below the line, my mantra for life might be "just work a little harder". I'm operating on the theory that hard work will generally equal leadership. I assume that if I just dig a little deeper, work a little harder, put in a few more hours, that I am leading. I assume that others will see how hard I'm working and follow me, rising to my high expectations that they do the same. This almost never happens, and this is not leadership. When someone operates solely below the line, it leads to an environment of frustration, burnout, bitterness, resentment... you get the idea.

The mistake of leading solely from below the line can also hurt our personal relationships, when we try to "busy" ourselves into a healthy relationship with another person. Our thought is that if we just fill our lives with things to do, places to be and projects to accomplish, the relationship will take care of itself. That is a recipe for relationship disaster.

Conversely, those who are only willing to operate above the line must realize how damaging this can be to others, and to their goals. Staying above the line results in promises that aren't kept, empty encouraging words, unmet expectations and unacceptable results. Staying above the line causes an individual to lose their credibility because often, when we only operate above the line, tasks go undone and nothing ever gets accomplished. A connection that is based on authenticity and trust that is developed above the line quickly dissipates if there is no action to back up the words that were promised. Likewise, a vision statement or mission statement (both "above the line" ideas) posted on the wall with no action backing them up does more damage to the team than if there were no vision and mission at all. Staying above the line all the time results in disappointment, lack of trust, frustration and discouragement.

In a personal relationship, choosing to always stay "above the line" might look like having lots of great conversations, but not following through on any of your promises. Your partner may feel a chemistry or a bond with you, but the lack of follow-through and mismatched actions will eventually lead to disillusionment and mistrust.

Conclusion

Remember, a below the line leader that only cares about accomplishing the task is not leading anything. After all, you lead people, not tasks.

And a leader who always stays above the line is full of empty promises and unmet goals and is not to be trusted to follow through.

It is this general inability of leaders to operate both above and below the line that led me to write this book. If you have read this far, I challenge you to join me as we explore how to effectively *lead people* above the line and *execute on goals* below the line. I cannot promise you that it will be comfortable or easy. I can promise that if you choose to become a student of leading above the line and executing below the line your relationships will improve both personally and professionally. Our inability to operate both above and below the line creates a huge gap in our leadership as well as in our relationships. Learning to bridge this gap takes intentionality, authenticity and hard work. It is not an easy task; it is a trained skill. I invite you to process, practically apply, debate and disagree with my comments. Don't take my word for it–try to apply these principles to your own life and see how they measure up.

CHAPTER 2

Crossing From Above
To Below The Line

Let's jump in and look at the leadership of those who have a tendency to be more comfortable hanging out "above the line". While it may appear to be fun, exciting, and inspiring to stay above the line in the land of building authentic relationships, motivating others, and crafting compelling visions, staying above the line all the time has devastating effects on the success of any relationship, team, or organization.

In today's world, we are constantly exposed to people who want to stay above the line. We hear political pundits expounding on the many problems we're facing and all of their solutions for solving them—and yet we rarely see effective action or real change from them. We are saturated with ads for self-help books that give us "five keys to success" or "four non-fail tips to better living". These kinds of tools are typically inspiring and motivating, and almost never backed up with the necessary accountability for behavior change that is needed to truly see results. Personally, we all know someone who talks a big game and is probably fun to be around, but who, more than once, has made promises that are ultimately never kept. These are all examples of staying above the line. The effects of staying above and refusing to cross below are similarly disappointing or even disastrous in a professional setting.

Meet Mark

Let me introduce you to Mark. Mark is the founder and CEO of a young tech startup, with a mission to improve the way people learn through the use of innovative technology. It's an inspiring mission, and Mark has built a team of passionate people that are willing to put in the long hours and brave the uncertainty that comes with any startup company because they believe in the vision, and they believe in him. In our Make A Difference personality language, Mark is a People-Loving Parrot with a secondary score of a Tranquil Turtle. Mark is a great speaker, has incredible interpersonal skills, and he's gotten his business and his team this far by inspiring the people he leads with his words and with the vision he is able to paint for them. Mark's success is largely based on his ability to build strong relationships with those around him.

However, after about two years of hustle and sporadic growth, things are beginning to break down. While the company itself is receiving rave reviews from its customers and being handed many opportunities to expand, Mark's team is beginning to burn out. There are complaints about the lack of structure or clear expectations, and the initial excitement and dedication to the cause is waning in the light of unmet goals and a lack of progress. There are even whispers that Mark himself is a phony, and full of "hot air"—that he doesn't mean what he says or back up his words with actions. Mark feels his team disengaging from the mission, and he is struggling to get them re-engaged and motivated to continue onwards through the chaos of his emerging company's unstructured growth. You see, Mark the Parrot/Turtle is an above the line leader, and he hasn't yet learned how to cross below the line.

When they begin to flounder, those who stay above the line are the ones that are often referred to as examples of poor, shallow leadership. While people-driven leadership sounds good on paper, building teams and creating culture without any execution of tasks or processes will ultimately only result in unfulfilled dreams and unmet goals. Those who always stay above the line will eventually experience a breakdown of their team's ability to trust their leadership, and thus a breakdown of their ability to progress their goals and move their organization forward. These frustrated leaders may refuse to cross the line and instead try to solidify their leadership by staying squarely above the line. They try to salvage their team's perception of them as a strong, effective leader. This never works in the long term. For instance, they may distance themselves from processes and procedures that are needed to ensure execution and accountability. Instead of executing, they pontificate with long speeches of "inspiration" and "encouragement". This causes the team to see the leader as having a lack of depth and leading solely with emotion and words instead of using solid structure and data.

You may have experienced the results of a leader who speaks eloquently about the relevance of their vision and the importance of their mission but lacks the ability to take action and create meaningful change. Confidence drops, trust plummets and integrity wains when we are subjected to the leadership of someone who over promises and under delivers, again and again.

Back to Mark's story. He realizes that he is losing trust with his team, and he understands that it's due to his inability to accomplish the big goals he has sold them. His leadership team in particular seems frustrated and their performance has been slipping. Even worse, their attitude towards Mark and mistrust in his leadership is becoming toxic and spreading throughout the organization. Mark is hurt; these people on his leadership team are not just his employees, they're his friends. He knows he needs to address the poor attitude and decline in performance, but he refuses to cross below the line and develop accountability and structure for his team. Unless he develops his leadership skills and chooses to use them to cross below the line, his team and ultimately his company will suffer.

At this point, Mark is unable to have the hard conversations necessary to hold his team members accountable for their performance. He has lost credibility and trust by making empty promises and setting ambiguous goals with no accountability, over and over again. His inability to follow through has done significant damage to his relationships with those he leads. Mark has tried to motivate his team back into alignment and action, holding meetings with agendas meant to remind them of their inspiring mission, and even hosting a few company-wide off-site retreats to try to re-engage and re-ignite his team's energy and passion, but to no avail. In fact, these efforts were seen by his team as placating, more empty words that wouldn't be followed up with action or lead to any real change in their culture or in their day-to-day lives.

You see, a result of staying above the line is that we lose the ability to initiate and hold an effective hard conversation—a conversation about unmet expectation, errors or mistakes, unwelcome changes, or unsatisfactory performance. These are the kinds of conversations that we would all rather avoid, but avoidance will only allow the issue to get worse. This usually looks like broaching the issue and stating the problems that you're seeing, but failing to take the next step of coming up with an action plan to address the issue and setting clear boundaries and consequences if the issue continues to persist and go unsolved. Bringing up how you feel and what you are observing in others is very important, but alone it is not enough to effect change. When there is no action or accountability to back up a hard conversation, it results in ineffective and inauthentic leadership, and often a loss of trust on both sides. So, hard conversations begin above the line and then the leader must cross the line to ensure action and accountability.

We see how detrimental staying above the line in your leadership can be. If you scored higher in an above the line personality type (our Parrots and Turtles) you may be about ready to throw in the towel and give up on this leadership thing. But remember, leadership is not a characteristic--it is a skill that can be practiced and honed by everyone. **Your personality type does not mandate how you must lead at all times**. Being an above the line personality type does not mean that you're doomed to the kind of ineffective, empty leadership that I've just described. In fact, throughout my career, I've watched above the line personality types lead teams not only effectively, but with excellence. We all must choose to get out of our own comfort zones in order to lead, and for above-the-liners, that means crossing below the line.

Creating Measured Execution

Take a look at this formula.

$$E + P + C = FA$$

$$\overline{}$$

$$G + D + A = ME$$

In order to bring clarity to leading above and below the line, I have developed an equation for each area. Above the line success begins with E + P + C = FA (**E**xpectations + **P**riorities + **C**ommitment = **F**ocused **A**lignment). I will discuss this in the next chapter. Below the line success is gained with implementing the equation **G + D + A = ME**. This stands for **Goals + Data + Accountability = Measured Execution**.

Goals + Data + Accountability = Measured Execution

Successful below the line leadership occurs when there is Measured Execution. The process of achieving ME begins with setting reasonable and attainable *Goals*. This includes looking at the above the line equation and making sure that your goals are aligned with the Expectations, Priorities and Commitments made above the line. Once again, we will dive into the above the line process in the next chapter. Setting the right goals is essential. Many leaders can set goals, fewer leaders take the time to cross the line to ensure the goals are aligned with the overall vision and mission of the team. For instance, narcissistic leaders may set goals that make themselves look good or they may set goals that further their personal agenda only. Successful goals are those that align with the vision of the organization and are aimed at what is best for the company and the team. They are reasonable and set in order to provide a compass for accomplishment within the organization. These types of goals can be achieved on multiple levels within the company. They are set with the intent to provide a tangible focus point or points for the team, company or organization. Setting successful goals takes time, process, collaboration and most of all clear communication. Goals that are unclear cause confusion and frustration. Solid goals yield focus, planning, and allow for effective process for performance.

Once the correct goals are established then you need accurate *Data*. This looks like creating a scorecard with relevant metrics. *Warning: make sure you are measuring the right things*. Take the time to create meaningful metrics that will give a forward and backward look at your progress. Your scorecard should be simple and should capture the relevant information you need to accomplish your goals. Looking back, data can be a record of progress in the last quarter, month, week or day. Forward looking data can be predictors of inventory, outcomes and performance. Goals should be carefully created with this question at the foremost of the process: "How is this data relevant to achieving our goals?" Data that has no purpose causes a lack of clarity and gives a false sense of success. True data gives targeted feedback that allows for adjustments and consistent movement toward the established goals.

The next step is one that will take discipline and consistency. I am referring to *Accountability*. This means taking the time to structure a system that allows for ownership, flexibility and correction in the execution process. If the data shows that you are off course from achieving your goals, then you must be willing to take responsibility for the failure or wrong direction. Next, you must be flexible enough to correct your process in order to get realigned with your goals. A lack of accountability drives complete failure and stagnation of a team or company. Successful accountability occurs when leaders realize that they will encounter obstacles and failures and allow themselves and their team to recognize these and adjust accordingly.

It is how we deal with difficulties that will define our ultimate success or failure as a leader.

This is true in our personal relationships as well. It looks like setting *goals* for a relationship, and then using *data* by developing a personal scorecard to see if we are tracking toward those goals. Finally, creating a*ccountability* in relationships is critical. Being willing to say "I'm sorry" or being willing to offer forgiveness are essential for effective relational accountability. These three components can help you to build stronger and more satisfying personal relationships.

In professional or personal relationships this simple equation, **Goals + Data + Accountability**, will result in the **Measured Execution** that allows us to lead successfully below the line.

Think about our previous example of Mark. While he may have been a natural above the line leader, he lacked skills in the process of truly being successful in the long term. Using the below the line equation is the first step in leading well for the "Marks" of the world. But it is only the first step.

————————————

Goals + **D**ata + **A**ccountability = **M**easured Execution

Now that you have learned how to cross from above to below the line, let's take a look at what it means to cross from below to above the line.

CHAPTER 3

Crossing From Below
To Above The Line

When I talk with leaders who are much more comfortable living below the line than above the line, I recognize a pattern. Generally, these leaders equate execution with leadership. One will tell me that the ultimate definition of leadership is accomplishing the task. Another will say that unless the goals are met, there is no leadership. The pattern is consistent—below the line leaders associate strong leadership with strong accomplishments. They find their purpose in the task at hand and evaluate the success of a leader on his or her ability "to take the hill". This seems to work for them, at least in the short-term, because they receive recognition and accolades for a job well done...or not. Therefore, they tend to judge those they lead simply by their ability to get things done.

If I broach the subject of culture, leading people well, encouraging others, building relationship and cohesiveness, the below the line leader's eyes began to dim and I can see the look of "oh boy, here we go again". This is the time when the below the line leaders checks out of the conversation because they have heard this before. "Now Larry is going to initiate his touchy feely, emotional leadership training," is going through their minds. Generally, they try to be nice, but it is obvious that when I begin talking about leading people instead of tasks they either politely disengage, become defensive, or simply endure the rest of the conversation. To the below the line leader, such talk about loyalty and team building and connecting have no place in the work environment. The below the line leaders believes that they have one purpose and that is to do the job that they have been hired to do. They become frustrated when anything gets in their way including the "soft skills" training that they are being subjected to during these conversations.

The truth is that choosing to be a below the line leader all of the time will bring the exact opposite results from what you are seeking. Living below the line may bring short-term wins but, in the long-term, creates an environment that is at best disconnected and at worst devastating. I have met with countless below the line leaders who have no clue why their employees are disengaged, frustrated and have low job satisfaction. Staying below the line is a sure recipe for failure as a leader.

I've had numerous conversations with men and women who serve in our military. Obviously, there are definitely below the line execution goals that must be met in order to protect our nation and secure our interests abroad. However, when I ask men who have served on the battlefield about leadership, I received a very interesting response. They tell me that there are leaders in the military that they respect because of the position that they hold, however they do not respect that leader as an influencer in their lives. There are other leaders that they have served, who continue to influence their lives to this very day. I've heard this described to me many times from many different active-duty men and women as well as veterans.

What is the difference between a leader who garners only respect for his position and accomplishments, and the leader who garners respect because of the impact that he has made on someone's life?

I believe the difference is knowing how to lead both below and above the line. This is a very difficult thing to do. It is easy for below the line leaders to get hyper focused on the task at hand. That is what drives them. That is what gives them energy. That is what truly validates the below the line leader. It is accomplishing the task with excellence. We must know and understand that research and data through the years have substantiated that only leading below the line is not the definition of leadership but instead is the definition of poor leadership.

Meet Shelly

Let me introduce you to Shelly. Shelly is a partner in an up-and-coming coffee house with a mission to provide an excellent experience for people who desire specialized coffee in a unique environment. It is a challenging mission and Shelly has built a team of driven, motivated people who are willing to work long hours and face stiff competition because they want to accomplish the task of making this company a national franchise success. In our Make A Difference personality language, Shelly is a Leading Lion with a secondary score of Competent Camel. Shelly is a highly motivated, hard worker with a big vision and strong organizational skills. Shelly has been successful with getting the business this far by using sheer muscle and having the ability to be a problem solver.

However, after a couple of years of working incredibly long hours, things are taking a downward turn. While the quality of the product is high and the overall business model is sound, something is not working. Her team is becoming disgruntled and customers are starting to give sour reviews on social media about the customer service. The team feels like they are robots who are expected to show up, work hard, go home and then report for duty the next day to do it all over again. They say that Shelly is rude and at times arrogant. Her lack of patience with the team is taking its toll. Shelly continues to demand more work and has no clue about the demise in the culture of her team. Shelly, the Lion/Camel is a below the line leader; she lacks the ability to cross above the line and lead her people.

When those who are below the line experience difficulty leading, they are often referred to as dominant, uncaring, and dictatorial. While task driven leaders can accomplish tangible goals in the short term, their lack of people skills often derails their leadership. Leading solely below the line breeds frustration, lack of teamwork, insecurity and discontentment. When a leader stays only below the line, they will eventually experience a downward spiral of a lack of engagement from the team and thus their ability to accomplish tasks and achieve their vision will greatly diminish. This may cause the frustrated leader who refuses to cross the line to dig in below the line and demand more from her team. She may accuse the team of being unwilling to work, and of even becoming unmotivated or lazy. This tactic never works in the long term. The leader may "double down" on accountability and execution. She may become cold and indifferent to individual needs. This causes the team to see this leader as having no empathy and only thinking of herself instead of creating a team environment and strong culture.

You may have experienced a leader who is driven, works hard and can accomplish tasks, but lacks the ability to lead people and create a buy-in on their team. Morale drops, distrust in motives rises, and an overall sense of burnout and a lack of purpose permeates the team.

Back to Shelly. She realizes that she is losing the ability to lead her team. She finally realizes that her gap in leadership has caused discontent and confusion. She becomes aware of the high level of frustration and overall overwhelmed feeling that has saturated her employees throughout her organization. In other words, her team is becoming toxic. Shelly is angry. She thought this team was a group of hard workers who knew how to get the job done. She knows something has gone wrong but refuses to cross the line and address the culture issues. Unless she develops her leadership skills and chooses to cross the line, her team and ultimately her company will suffer.

At this point, Shelly is unable to motivate her team to provide great customer service and work with excellence. She has lost credibility and trust by increasing her demands and by what her team calls micromanaging the tasks. Her inability to inspire and create an atmosphere of teamwork is causing serious employee and morale concerns. Her effort to fix the problem by dictating and demanding more has been ineffective and damaging. She even created work score cards and spreadsheets to track performance. All of her below the line efforts were to no avail. In fact, these efforts were seen by Shelly's team as a way for her to squeeze more work out of them in order to achieve her own agenda.

A result of staying below the line is that we lose the ability to inspire and connect with our team. Inspiring our team does not mean lofty speeches or lectures. It means demonstrating authentic care for each person you lead. It means choosing to invest with your time, energy and emotion. It is sending a clear picture that your team is more important than the task at hand. It looks like putting a personal connection item on the agenda of each team member, checking in with their personal lives with sincere care. Many below the line leaders struggle with connecting with their team. They are uncomfortable with the intangible process of building a strong culture. Many struggle with the ability to demonstrate authentic concern. Choosing to learn how to develop and motivate a team by crossing to lead above the line while executing below the line is the secret to success.

Remember from our previous chapter that leadership is not a characteristic—it is a skill that can be learned and improved. Your personality type does not mandate how you must lead. Being a below the line personality type does not mean that you are locked into the demanding micro-managing leadership that I've just described. In fact, I know those who are naturally below the line leaders who have learned the skill of crossing the line and they are highly effective and successful leaders. We, like these leaders must choose to get out of our own comfort zones in order to lead. For the below the line leaders this means crossing the line in order to develop your skills above the line.

Creating Focused Alignment

Remember our diagram? In order to bring clarity to leading above and below the line, I have developed an equation for each area. In the previous chapter we have discussed the below the line equation of G + D + A = ME. Now let's take a look at the above the line equation. Above the line success begins with **E + P + C = FA.**

$$E + P + C = FA$$

Successful above the line leadership occurs when there is *Focused Alignment*. The process of achieving FA begins with developing and communicating *Expectations*. This includes creating vision, attitudes, communication rhythms, conflict rules, values, mission, authenticity, honesty and transparency for the team or relationship. Know that this is not an exhaustive list and you will want to define the expectations for your professional and personal relationships.

Once the expectations are established, you must then develop your *Priorities.* This means taking your expectations and prioritizing what is most important to the team or relationship. For instance, if communication is the most important it would be listed as number one and if transparency was not as important it would be listed near the bottom of the expectation list. This creates a realistic look at what the team should focus on and in what order.

The next step is one that many choose to skip. This is a fatal mistake as this piece is absolutely essential to successfully creating Focused Alignment. I am referring to *Commitment.* Many choose to overlook the importance of getting buy-in from those you lead. While setting expectations and priorities are nice, they are meaningless unless they are undergirded with commitment. This looks like taking the top 3 priorities (attempting to focus on more can lead to a diluted and unfocused process) and asking the team to write their commitments to each expectation. In our previous example, if communication was the top priority, then you would ask the members of your team to make a commitment of one or two things they were willing to do to increase communication effectiveness. For instance, someone might commit to communicating each week through an email on the overall progress of their area. In a personal relationship, if authenticity was a top priority, one might commit to make their relationship partner aware when they were frustrated or anxious.

When we follow this simple equation: **Expectations + Priorities + Commitment** the result will be **Focused Alignment** that allows us to lead successfully above the line.

Think about our previous example of Shelly. While she may have been a natural below the line leader, she lacked the people skills of truly being successful in the long term. Using the above the line equation is the first step in leading well for the "Shellys" of the world. But it is only the first step.

Expectations + **P**riorities + **C**ommitment = **F**ocused **A**lignment

---

CHAPTER 4

Breaking It Down

Let's dig a little deeper into this concept of leading above and below the line. We know that there are leaders who are more comfortable above the line, and those who are more comfortable below the line. We can gain a more in-depth understanding of how to lead and connect with both types of leaders as well as those in our personal relationships by taking a look at the four personality types that were discussed earlier in this book.

By now, you should know your personality type and I hope that you have thought about what happens when you move from one personality quadrant to another. Most people have a primary and secondary personality, and our behavior can change due to our environment or current situation in which we are operating.

It is important to have an understanding of each of the personality types as they relate to leading "above the line" versus "below the line". This knowledge is important for increasing your own self-awareness so that you can become a stronger leader. But perhaps it's more important for you to gain this knowledge so that you can better lead those around you. Taking the time to increase your awareness concerning diverse personalities allows you to leverage your newly gained insights in the professional and personal relationship settings.

In this section of the book, I'd like you to challenge yourself to grow deeper and stronger as a leader. Dive into the content, take time to think about its application in your life and use the information to build better relationships with those within your circle of influence. Stretch your mind and develop a new way of communicating, leading, and investing in those you care about.

People-Loving Parrot

Parrots naturally want to fly around "above the line". Because they are social creatures their strength is many times found in their ability to use their words. They tend to be verbal communicators and many times they will "think with their mouth". Verbal processing can be a good thing or a bad thing, depending on the context. When a Parrot interacts with those who lead below the line, their constant verbal thinking can cause confusion or even frustration and may ultimately hinder the progress and success of the team.

*What Parrots need to know to be successful **below the line:***

> The Parrot must realize that the strength of their words may actually become a weakness when they are working and leading below the line. What seems like a positive and natural way to communicate and collaborate can come across as unproductive, confusing, or a waste of time. The Parrot needs to realize that below the line is not a place for brainstorming, dreaming, or visioning. They must discipline themselves to focus on process, execution and follow-through.

> When leading below the line, the Parrot must come to grips with the fact that their words may not be helpful or appreciated. It is their responsibility to learn how to speak the below the line language of spreadsheets, metrics and accountability measurements. They will need to discipline themselves to stay focused on the tasks that are critical to the project and enable their team members to make progress and get the job done. Demonstrating consistency, reliability, and rigor may not be easy but it is essential for the Parrot to be successful leading any team in any organization.

> Perhaps the most concise way to describe what a Parrot needs to know in order to be successful below the line

is this: it will not be fun, enjoyable, or even fulfilling. However, it is necessary to develop the disciplines of leading below the line if you want to accomplish goals and gain credibility with others.

If you are a Parrot attempting to lead below the line, this will not be an easy thing to accomplish. It will take time, energy and much effort to practice working within a structure or process, executing on tasks, and analyzing data on a consistent basis. The Parrot should use their strengths to help them accomplish or refine their below the line skills. They should use their communication skills to increase their understanding of the expectations of those who are operating below the line. They should use their natural people skills to create connections that will help them to understand the demand, stress and needs of those below the line. Leveraging their ability to lead with agility and flexibility will be a real asset in expanding their leadership scope below the line.

What Parrots Need to Remember:

When the Parrot is working with or leading a below the line Lion, it is best to remember to communicate with large rocks of bullet points instead of multiple pebbles with many words. This means get to the point. Speak in definitive terms of "I can"," or I will", instead of "I'm not sure" or "maybe". Lions need Parrots to be less dramatic and more pointed. The Parrot needs to put away their sensitivity and not allow the Lion's direct words to hurt their feelings. The Parrot needs to remember to not waste time trying to get the Lion to like them. *Just work with the Lion to get the job done!*

When the Parrot is working with or leading a below the line Camel, the name of the game is details. The Parrot must be disciplined to value preparation and display an affinity for the small tasks that must be accomplished. This will be a real challenge for the Parrot as generally they disdain details and find them incredibly boring. The Parrot must put in the time and effort to be prepared before meetings and more importantly, allow the Camel to bring their detailed data to the table. Camels need the Parrot to be less impulsive and more process driven. The Parrot needs to remember that the logical Camel will not get or appreciate their humor. *Just deal in black and white facts please!*

When the Parrot is working with or leading an above the line Turtle, her high energy is a detriment to authentic communication. Presenting with a calm demeanor and providing time for thoughtful responses from a Turtle is key. Bombarding the Turtle with a ton of information and demanding a quick answer is a sure way to build frustration and resentment in the Turtle. The Parrot should give the Turtle time to process and consider using less verbal and more written communication. Turtles need Parrots to turn down the emotion and take the time to have a meaningful thoughtful conversation. *Just slow down and think before you act.*

The above information should be applied to personal and professional relationships. In fact, if the Parrot is going to grow as a leader, it must be applied to both. The Parrot who uses these concepts at home as well as at work will find their relationships significantly improving. Learning what others need from us is crucial to growing meaningful relationships.

If this sounds like a lot of work, it is. Leading others based on their personality style, takes intentional preparation, knowledge, and a lot of determination. When the Parrot leads or journeys out of their personality quadrant, they expend a ton of energy. It is important to allow yourself to have sufficient "Parrot time" of having fun and enjoying people so that you don't burn out in the process of leading others.

The reward of becoming an impactful influencer is worth the effort. Parrots, don't get overwhelmed or discouraged when you fail at leading others effectively. Use the failing as a learning experience. Be determined to grow your leadership and relationship muscles. You have great natural leadership skills; I challenge you to take the next step of developing the discipline of leading outside of your natural habitat.

Leading Lion

Lions naturally roam below the line. They are not social creatures, and their strength is found in the ability to accomplish their task. They tend to be action oriented and therefore can make quick decisions. However, those decisions may not always be wise. The Lion does not need collaboration or discussion. They need to know the end expectation or result that is required. When a Lion ventures above the line, he can cause destruction, chaos and anger by his lack of tact and poor communication skills.

*What Lions need to know to be successful **above the line:***

The Lion must realize that his strength of accomplishing the task could actually become a weakness when working and leading above the line. What seems to be a very positive and natural way to lead below the line may come across as rude, arrogant and even unproductive. The Lion needs to realize that above the line is not a place for the head down, execution at all cost, philosophy. They must discipline themselves to focus on improving their people skills which will ultimately help to accomplish their tasks. When leading above the line, the Lion must create a vision outside of their own value stream. It is their responsibility to learn how to lead and support those who think differently above the line.

This means that the Lion will need to get comfortable with verbal affirmation, collaboration, and team building. They will need to discipline themselves to refrain from dominating others with their direct and sometimes bossy attitude. Demonstrating patience, people skills, teamwork, and self-awareness may not come naturally but it is essential for the Lion to be successful leading an organization above the line.

While a Lion may feel that leading above the line is frivolous, nonproductive, and frustrating, that is not true. It will be necessary to develop the discipline of leading above the line if the Lion is going to gain respect and credibility from those team members who live and lead above the line.

Certainly, this is not an easy task to accomplish. Developing the skills to lead above the line will take time, energy and much effort. The Lion should use their strength of vision to create goals designed to improve their above the line leading skills. They should use their natural leadership skill of perseverance and determination to create rigor and rhythm above the line. Leveraging their ability to tackle difficult tasks will propel their leadership scope above the line.

What Lions Need to Remember:

When a Lion is working with or leading a below the line Camel, they must remember that the "devil is in the details". In other words, the Lion must choose to honor the process of discovering and working through the details. Because the Lion loves to fly at 30,000 feet, this will be a real challenge. Putting the time and effort into preparing and allowing for data to be processed appropriately means slowing down the Lion's agenda which is solely to "get it done". Below the line for the Camel means process and for the Lion it means accomplishing the task. Just as important as it is for the Lion to be prepared with details is the ability of that Lion to allow the Camel to bring questions, data and more questions to the table. The Lion needs to remember that the Camel does not appreciate big picture thinking that does not contain appropriate detailed information. *Just honor the details and answer the questions.*

When the Lion is leading the above the line Turtle, they must remember to put their high powered, fast moving leadership gear in neutral. The Lion's driven and demanding personality will quickly shutdown their Turtle colleagues. Presenting with meaningful dialogue and questions for the Turtle will yield effective results. Building a successful relationship with the Turtle will not be accomplished on the Lion's timetable. The Lion must remember to adjust their timetable to meet the needs of the Turtle. Also, the Lions must refrain from accusing the Turtle of being weak because they move a bit slower than the Lions. Remember, speed has nothing to do with strength. Turtles need Lions to back off of the throttle, remember your tone, and learn to listen. *Just don't be rude.*

When the Lion is leading the above the line Parrot, they must remember that words are king. This means they should allow the Parrot to think out loud without receiving judgment or condemnation. Remember that to the Parrot, many words are necessary for creating solid decisions that lead to action. Parrots need Lions to be less intolerant and pointed with their language. Lions need to work on being more aware of how they are perceived by the Parrot who lives above the line.

A kind gesture, a smile or a word of appreciation from the Lion will go a long way toward building respect and credibility with the Parrot. The Lion needs to remember that people skills are a choice. *Just relax and smile every now and then.*

It is important for the below the line Lion to remember to apply these principles in their personal and professional lives if they are going to grow and truly be effective as leaders. Lions may unknowingly have damaged relationships all around them. Practical application of crossing the line concepts is vital for those relationships to heal or become healthy. Using them at home as well as at work will be difficult for the Lion but necessary for true leadership and relationship growth.

The above information may seem impossible or incredibly difficult. This should not discourage the Lion but should motivate them to determine to accomplish this feat. It will take perseverance, determination, knowledge and time. When the Lion chooses to venture out of his personality quadrant there is a cost. Even Lions can run out of energy when leading from an uncomfortable place. Make sure that you spend enough time in your Lion quadrant to "conquer a few hills" in order to renew your energy.

The reward of growing your influence as a leader is certainly worth the work it takes to get there. Lions, be sure not to expect quick success, and be cognizant of becoming frustrated or angry when you don't see the results that you desire. Use your failures as opportunities to grow and be determined to persevere until you are comfortable being uncomfortable as a leader. It is a huge challenge, but I know that you are up to the task.

Competent Camel

The natural habitat of the Camel is squarely below the line. They are very logical, and their strength is the ability to create data and focus on details. They tend to be process driven and therefore use linear thinking to make decisions. While appropriate in some cases, linear thinking can also result in decisions that are not flexible or agile. The Camel does not need humor or connection to feel validated. They need to know the details. They need information and a lot of it. When Camels journey across the wilderness into the above the line environment, they can cause resentment, frustration and insecurity by their constant questioning and, at times, their critical nature.

*What Camels need to know to be successful **above the line:***

> The Camel must realize that his strength of processing details can actually become a weakness when working and leading above the line. What seems to be very helpful below the line may come across as critical and negative above the line. The Camel needs to realize that the above the line environment is not a place for black and white thinking or concrete detailed answers. They must discipline themselves to improve their people skills by becoming comfortable with the ambiguous language and lifestyle of those above the line. When leading above the line, Camels may leverage their ability to process and create a tangible method for connecting with consistency. It will be their responsibility to learn how to lead and support those above the line people who they do not understand.

> This means that Camels will need to begin the process of learning how to interpret and respond to the feelings and abstract behavior of their above the line colleagues. They must be aware not to overly criticize or present with a negative attitude. Demonstrating an appreciation for humor, big picture thinking, soft skills, and intangible ideas are some of the qualities

that must be developed. It will not be easy, but it is entirely necessary if the Camel is going to be successful leading a team or organization.

While a Camel may feel that leading above the line is unnecessary, confusing, unorganized and ambiguous, this is not true. It will be necessary to develop the discipline of leading above the line if Camels are going to gain credibility and respect from their peers, leaders, family or friends who lead above the line.

I realize that this is not easy. Developing the skills to lead above the line will take focus, planning, preparation and intentional effort. Camels should use their strength to help create specific action steps designed to grow their above the line leading skills to the next level. They should use their natural ability of process to create a consistent and stable investment above the line. Leveraging the ability to sustain rhythm and accuracy will greatly help to grow their leadership muscle above the line.

What Camels need to remember:

When Camels are working with or leading an above the line Parrot, they must remember that nothing is concrete. This means that you should allow the Parrot to think creatively without boxing the Parrot into a corner of logic and reason. Remember that creative thinking and talking are essential to the Parrot's ability to feel validated and appreciated. That creativity can lead to productivity if developed appropriately. Parrots need Camels to be conscious of squelching ideas or brainstorming activities with black-and-white, logical thought processing. Camels should work on creating an awareness of how they may be perceived by the Parrot as a critical, always say "no", person. An encouraging word, an appreciation

33

for humor, and an act of gratitude will go a long way toward building respect and credibility with the Parrot. The Camel needs to remember that developing greater people skills is a process. *Just stop nitpicking and expect the unexpected.*

When Camels are leading a below the line Lion, they must remember that the Lion has only one set of eyeglasses and they only see things from the long range of 30,000 feet. In other words, Camels must choose to get out of the weeds if they are going to be successful at leading the Lion. Allowing the Lion to roar with vision and valor without squelching his mission is the difficult assignment of the Camel. This will take much thought and preparation by the Camel. They must create a mindset that allows for big picture thinking, big rock talking and big action planning. The Camel needs to remember that the Lion does not appreciate the details and should be careful to only saturate the Lion with essential information. The Camel must rebuke the temptation to fully explain and process data to the Lion. This will be quite a challenge but quite effective. *Just get out of the weeds and give the big picture.*

When Camels are leading the above the line Turtle, they must remember to put their love for tons of analytical data aside. Their need to feed the data beast will result in a mass of polarizing, slow responses from their Turtle colleagues. Presenting with meaningful questions and thoughtful dialogue will allow the above the line Turtle to connect and contribute to the project at hand. Building a successful relationship with the Turtle takes time and will not happen quickly. However, the time investing in the relationship will be well spent. The Camel can help the Turtle by creating deadlines and then creating checkpoints leading up to the deadlines. The Camel must be careful not to create unrealistic expectations for the Turtle that will lead to frustration and anxiety. Turtles need Camels to create a calm stable relationship that is based on trust. *Just cut the amount of data down and take the first step.*

It is important for below the line Camels to remember that the above concepts are to be used in their personal and professional life if they are going to grow their relationship and leadership skills. The Camel may not be aware of the frustration people feel when they struggle to have a meaningful relationship with that Camel. It will not be easy to apply some of these principles at home as well as at work, but it is absolutely necessary in order for true leadership and relationship growth to take place.

Camels, as you review the above content, it may seem very difficult or even unattainable. This should not discourage you but should encourage you to create a solid detailed leadership growth plan. The more difficult the task, the more important the process is to the equation. It will take process, perseverance, knowledge and time to realize the benefit of leading above and below the line.

When Camels choose to begin the process of venturing out of their personality quadrant, they must remember the cost. Leading outside of your own quadrant creates a depletion of energy that will lead to burnout frustration and even depression. Make sure that as a Camel you spend adequate "Camel time" by processing, planning and executing below the line. This will renew your energy level so that you can continue to effectively lead others.

The reward of growing your influence and leadership ability of those who are quite different than you is long-lasting. While it takes much work, and is not a quick process, it is completely worth the investment. You will fail in some of your efforts. That is not only okay, it is expected. Use those times of failure to learn how to strengthen your determination to grow as leader. You have the natural processing skills and consistency to exponentially increase your skill as leader. Now is the time to begin the process.

Tranquil Turtle

Turtles are above the line creatures. However, they're not social like their above the line counterparts, the Parrots. They are driven by one-on-one interpersonal connections. Turtles tend to be thoughtful and slow decision-makers. This can pose a problem when a quick decision is needed. The Turtle values collaboration and discussion especially when it is one-on-one. They need time to think and process internally and have the ability to look at a problem from several different angles. When Turtles choose to venture under the line, they can cause stagnation, a lack of communication and high frustration from their poor communication and slow-moving action.

*What Turtles need to know to be successful **below the line:***

Turtles must realize that their strength of wisdom and thoughtful conversation can actually become a weakness when working and leading below the line. What's seems to be a very positive and useful way of looking at things may come across as polarizing, apathetic, and ineffective below the line. The Turtle needs to realize that below the line is not a place for long philosophical thoughts and conversation. It is a place of action and execution. They must discipline themselves to focus on improving their ability to act quickly and communicate verbally. When leading below the line the Turtle must operate in a higher gear and be okay with not having the time to fully vet and think through every situation. It is the responsibility of the Turtle to learn how to support and lead those who think very differently below the line.

This means that the Turtle will need to get comfortable with talking more, moving faster, and taking calculated risks. They will need to discipline themselves to reframe from slowing down the process by being indecisive. Demonstrating an ability to make a solid decision in the proper amount of time, creating crucial conversations, and appreciating those who are task driven will not come naturally nor will it be easy. However, it will be essential for the Turtle to do these things in order to be successful at leading an organization or team below the line.

Perhaps the most effective way to describe what a Turtle needs to know, in order to be successful below the line, is that it may seem intimidating, overwhelming, out of control, and frustrating. Don't believe those myths. The truth is that it is necessary for Turtles to develop the discipline of leading below the line if they are going to gain and maintain the respect and credibility from those who lead below the line.

While this is not an easy task to accomplish it is important. Developing the skills to lead below the line will take courage, energy and effort. Turtles should use their strengths to create strong trusting relationships below the line. They should use their natural leadership skill of intentional thinking to create a solid plan aimed squarely at leading below the line. Leveraging their ability to persevere and endure difficult things will be a huge advantage as they expand their leadership scope under the line.

What Turtles need to remember:

When Turtles are working with and leading an above the line Parrot, they must remember that Parrots need energy. This means that they should allow the Parrot to bring creative energy and enthusiasm to the table. This also means that Turtles should affirm that energy and engage in the process of connecting with the Parrot. This looks like Turtles coming out of their shell and embracing the multiple words and energy of the Parrot. Remember that Parrots are looking for facial expression and nonverbal behavior. Parrots need Turtles to speak with their face as well as with words. The Turtle needs to work on not presenting with a flat affect that can be perceived as apathy. Showing interest and approval are essential keys to gaining the Parrot's trust and loyalty. The Turtle needs to remember that engaging with others is a choice. *Just crank up the volume of energy and engage!*

When a Turtle is working with or leading a below the line Lion, it is best to remember that Lions are incredibly action oriented. This means that the speed of the Turtle can greatly frustrate the Lion. Lions need Turtles to communicate quickly with direct language. This is most uncomfortable for the Turtle. However, they must keep their head out of their shell and lead the Lion with strong communication. Turtles must be ready to confront when necessary. While this may seem counterproductive to the Turtle, the Lion actually needs healthy confrontation from time to time. This sends a signal to the Lion that the Turtle is capable and strong enough to lead. The Lion respects and expects strength. Turtles must be prepared for the Lion's direct and even rude comments and not allow the Lion's aggressive nature to intimidate or dominate them. The Turtle needs to remember not to expect the Lion to slow down to a pace that is acceptable for the Turtle. *Just be direct and tell the Lion what you need.*

When Turtles are working with or leading a below the line Camel, they must remember that deadlines are rules and rules are meant to be kept. The Turtle must choose to respect the Camel's need for following rules. Camels live in a black-and-white world while Turtles live in a relatively gray world. Therefore, the Turtle must choose to develop an appreciation for following the process and rules that are important to the below the line Camel. This will be a real challenge for Turtles, and it will require that they develop a discipline for deadlines and details. The Turtle must remember that the Camel expects them to do exactly what they promised in the precise amount of time that was agreed upon. Turtles must allow the Camel to present in a detailed format and they must respond in an organized, outlined and detailed way. Turtles will be most effective leading the Camel by leveraging their dependability and consistency. *Just don't overpromise and under deliver.*

The above content should be applied on a personal and professional level if the Turtle is going to grow and develop successful relationships as a leader. There may be those who are not engaging the Turtle because they feel like the Turtle doesn't care or isn't interested. Turtles who choose to use these concepts at home as well as at work will find their relationships significantly deeper and stronger. Developing an understanding of what others need is crucial to developing meaningful relationships.

From the Turtle's perspective this probably sounds like a lot of work. The truth is it is a lot of work. Leading others based on their personality style will take courage, intention, preparation and determination. When Turtles choose to venture out of their personality quadrant there is a cost. Leading outside of your own quadrant expends incredible energy. This can lead to burnout, frustration and even depression. It is important to allow yourself to have sufficient "Turtle time" so that you can renew your energy and your soul.

Becoming a person of influence carries great reward. Turtles, allow me to encourage you not to become discouraged or overwhelmed when you fail at this process. You will fail because we all fail. Choose to use that failure as a learning experience. Allow it to help you grow and increase your determination to become a stronger more effective leader above and below the line. Use your natural leadership skill of creating authentic relationships to help you connect with those below the line. I challenge you to take a step out of your comfort zone and begin the process of leading at the next level and influencing others.

There you have it. Now you know what each personality needs to be successful above and below the line. This content is the foundation of being a successful leader and developing healthy successful relationships. I encourage you to take this section of the book and review it often. Use this as a resource for remembering what you need to do as well as a reminder of the needs of those who are in a different personality quadrant.

Why don't you take a minute right now and see if you can identify your relationships with others both above and below the line. I challenge you to begin the process of leading and connecting in an authentic and more meaningful way.

CHAPTER 5

The Monster

The question that keeps coming to my mind is: why do people not naturally choose to lead above and below the line? Why don't they make the decision to reach across their quadrant, take a risk, and connect with those who are different? Aren't our relationships important enough to do this? Isn't being effective and productive in our work environment enough of a priority to try leading differently?

As I have worked with companies and teams throughout the years, including mine, I've become aware of a monster. This monster prohibits relationships from growing, teams from connecting, and organizations from reaching their full potential. No one is immune. I've seen it attack and defeat large corporations, midsize companies, nonprofit organizations, churches, small companies, and personal relationships.

I believe this villainous creature has no bounds. It will devour and destroy anyone, or anything at any time. It has been around since the beginning of time yet almost always catches people by surprise. Given the right circumstances, environment, and culture, this Monster can thrive and eliminate anything in its path.

The name of the monster... is FEAR.

All of us have experienced it at one time or another in our life. It drives our behavior and many times our decisions. I believe it is the reason that leaders do not choose to cross the great divide that separates above and below the line individuals.

I personally have experienced the consequences of making decisions based out of fear instead of solid data and wise thought processing. Several years ago, our organization was experiencing a significantly steep growth curve. In hindsight, we were probably growing too fast with no solid infrastructure in place. Because I was afraid that we would not be able to keep the growth going at the current pace, I decided to bring on new employees at an alarmingly fast rate. My criteria for hiring was if they were breathing and had a pulse, they qualified! You can imagine what kind of results came from this hiring strategy. Then, I brilliantly made another decision to fix the problem. My solution was to take the new bad hires to lunch and tell them that they were terminated. What a horrible strategy! It didn't take very many lunches until the word got out in our company... "whatever you do, don't go to lunch with Larry!" Thankfully, our leadership team led me to slow down and we built a solid hiring process that led to sustained growth of the company. I learned a valuable lesson. It was to never make decisions out of fear. My poor decisions made out of fear, caused damage to our team and to those we hired who were not a good fit. I allowed the monster to wreak havoc and drive my behavior.

So, what is the answer to defeating this monster called fear? I believe it can be summed up with one word.... TRUST.

It appears to me that authentic trust has become a rarity in our business and personal relationships. We live in a world that thrives on causing fear and then offering ways to increase our security in every phase of our life. Because of the fear of criminals, we need sophisticated high-tech locks in our homes, our automobiles, businesses, computers, phones etc., etc.... There appear to be threats everywhere. One of the fastest growing markets today is cyber security. We are afraid of those who would steal our information and identity and do us harm.

Today's environment has provided a paranoid, fear driven, don't trust anyone mindset. It has caused us to isolate our lives into a security bubble that keeps us looking over our shoulder, no matter where we are or where we go. Truthfully, the fear is not unfounded. Through our access to social media and technology, we regularly see and hear of crime events, shootings, murders, theft, deception, and the list goes on and on.

It would be foolish not to take advantage of security technology that can help keep our families and our organizations safe. However, I believe we have taken that same fear mindset and applied it to our relationships. We know that people will deceive and hurt us, so we must not trust them. We buy into the fear that the best way to overcome the chance of being hurt is to protect ourselves at all costs.

This thought process keeps us cocooned in our personality quadrant and unwilling to risk the unknown of venturing above or below the line. Therefore, teams are formed in silos, organizations stay in protect-mode between divisions, and relationships stay at the surface level only. When this happens, fear rules the culture and decisions of the team or organization. Personally, fear causes relationships to stagnate.

The opposite of what I described above is gullibility. Wikipedia describes gullibility as: "a failure of social intelligence in which a person is easily tricked or manipulated into an ill-advised course of action." I am not advocating for gullible blind trust. That would be foolish. Trust given without merit or process is just plain stupid. There have been many who chose to trust in an ill-advised and toxic relationship. Those relationships always end up harmful, hurtful and generally do not last.

In the corporate world blind trust can devastate a company or organization. Trusting the wrong business partner or leader is a sure recipe for failure. Trusting the wrong people in your personal life will cause you to make bad decisions that will produce bad consequences.

If being overly vigilant results in polarization and isolation and being gullible results in disaster, what is the answer? I believe the answer is that we must not allow ourselves to fall into all or none thinking. We must be wise with how we approach the issue of trust. Specifically, I believe that trust is a process that is developed and grown. It is not a one-time event.

I suspect that the biggest reason for someone not to experience trust is because he or she has not chosen to trust the most important person in his or her life. That person is themselves. Trust begins with you. In other words, do you trust yourself?

If we do not trust ourselves, how can we build trust in others? Many times, we overlook this important step in building trust in others. Learning to trust ourselves is a process, just as building trust in a relationship or team is a process.

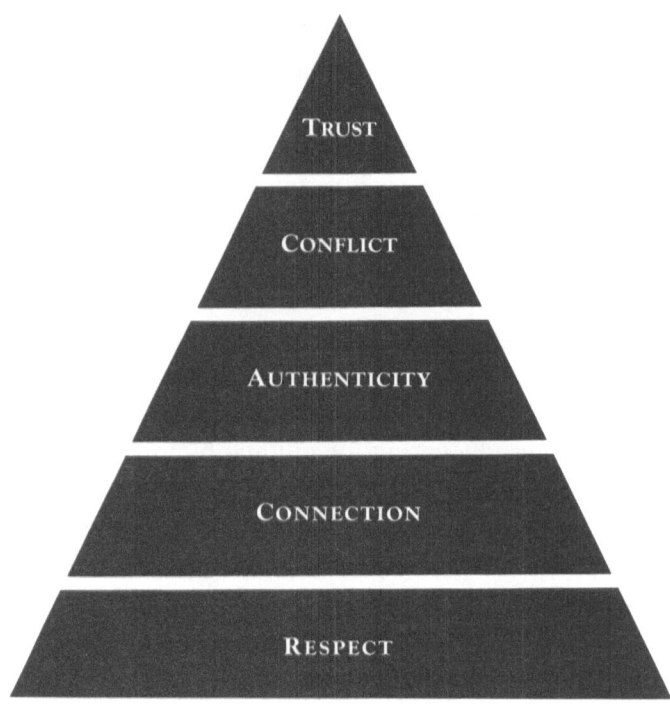

The Trust Triangle

Let's take a look at what I call the trust triangle. As I conducted research on the topic of trust, I discovered that many experts say a team should begin with trust and it should be the foundation of a relationship or team. I disagree. I believe trust, true trust, is earned over time and through experience. I do not believe that you can begin a relationship or a team with trust. Trust given without a process is equal to blind trust. Blind trust is rarely a good thing. This includes trusting ourselves.

Simply saying that we trust ourselves without going through the discipline of building self-trust is just empty words. Self-trust is gained through life experiences, good and bad decisions, and choosing to learn from both. Trusting yourself is something that you can grow and develop. It is a process.

I believe the foundation of trusting yourself is **respect**. It is the beginning of the process. Here is an important question: Is respect something that you earn or is respect something that you give yourself? How you answer this question may help you to understand more about how you process trust.

If you answered that respect must be earned, then you probably believe that it can also be lost. The problem with this answer concerning self-respect is that getting in the loop of earning and losing respect for yourself can be devastating. There is no doubt that the act of respect is something that can be gained or lost. However, the value of respecting ourselves as human beings is not something we should have to earn.

Certainly, we can act disrespectfully. We can lose respect because of our behavior. But the foundational value of respecting ourselves as unique, valued human beings is a choice. It is not earned, it is chosen. Choosing to respect our selves is the first step in developing self-trust.

Self-respect looks like choosing to set boundaries and guardrails in our lives. It means knowing that respect at the basic level begins with self-care, physically and emotionally. Physically, it means knowing what my body needs and taking the steps to provide those things. Emotionally, it means not allowing others to disrespect you with their words or behavior. Distancing yourself from those who spew abuse and do not respect you as a person is essential to developing self-respect.

Here is the take-away truth: you cannot expect anyone to respect you more than you are willing to respect yourself.

The decision is yours and it is important. Make the choice to take the first step and respect yourself.

The next step in the process of trusting yourself is to develop the ability to **connect** with your heart and soul. Many people go through life disengaged from being self-aware. They are not connected to their feelings or emotions.

Some people only use a very limited range of feelings or emotions. They may overuse anger, shame, defensiveness or being numb on the inside. They download these feelings over and over as way to cope with the difficulties of life. I am in no way minimizing or downplaying the incredible struggles that so many people go through every day. However, our brain allows us to access a plethora of emotions at any given time.

The problem is that we do not allow ourselves to connect with those feelings. That lack of self-awareness causes us to become disconnected from those around us. Realizing that our emotions and feelings are a vital part of our ability to navigate to successful relationships is important. Self-awareness is not only critical in our personal lives it is essential to successful business relationships.

In today's economy, those who understand how to create and maintain successful business relationships are the ones who experience success. No matter in what business you find yourself, the ability to develop strong relationships is essential. Relationships begin with understanding how to connect to your own feelings and emotions.

Let's be honest, many people do not like to think about their feelings or emotions. It is much easier for them to just push their feelings away. It is like they have a trashcan located next to their heart and as difficult things happen, they simply put their thoughts and feelings in the trashcan. The problem is that they have no connection so they cannot empty the trash can. What happens when a trashcan is overfilled and never taken out? The smell becomes unbearable. Likewise, when we do not know how to connect and deal with our feelings and emotions, they simply become stored away in the recesses of our heart. As hard as we try, we cannot keep those difficult feelings from building up and eventually spilling out.

It is essential that we develop skills and abilities that will allow us to honestly connect with our own hearts and process our feelings and emotions in a healthy way. This is not a "soft skill", this is a very hard skill. It takes determination and intentionality and most of all courage.

Some may need to solicit the help of a professional in order to become self-aware and gain the appropriate skills to process their emotion. Others may need simply to take the time to take an honest look in the mirror and allow their heart and mind to connect. There are a number of books written about how to become self-aware that would serve as good resources for you.

The third step in climbing the trust triangle is **authenticity.** Are you a person who is viewed as being authentic? Are you the same when times are good as well as when times are bad? Do you possess core values that drive your behavior and your lifestyle?

Being authentic does not mean that you have to be right all the time. It simply means that you are you, all the time. Obviously, we must behave differently in diverse environments. Don't misinterpret authenticity for bad judgment. Knowing how to navigate various situations, environments and cultures is the strength of a solid leader. However, they do not change who they are at the core of their being, regardless of the environment or circumstance.

Do you have non-negotiables in your life? Are there things that you will not compromise or change? These are the things that define who you are, what you believe, and where you're going. I understand that as we learn and grow, our beliefs may change. But we should not allow our beliefs to change with every new trend or scheme.

Having a foundation for your life means discovering the nonnegotiable values that will drive your decisions and ultimately your life. The process of developing self-trust has to include this critical component. If you do not know who you are, how can you trust yourself?

An authentic person is one who has the ability to remain the same in times of pressure and progress. You may not agree with him, but you know who he is and for what he stands. She may be unpredictable in some areas, but when it comes to knowing who she is and what she stands for, there is no doubt.

This doesn't mean that we always behave in a way that is consistent with our core values. Being authentic means realizing when we make mistakes and having the integrity to own those mistakes. Authentic simply means not to pretend.

Being authentic does not equal insensitivity. Someone who is determined to make a point or prove his case is not necessarily authentic. He is obnoxious. Authenticity begins in the heart and ends with our behavior. It has been my experience that those who exhibit authenticity have a powerful skill of connecting and building trust with others.

Being authentic to yourself means not allowing yourself to buy into the lie that you must be all things to all people. Personal authenticity begins with a humble confidence in knowing who you are and why you are. In other words, being confident in your purpose and value is where authenticity begins.

Authenticity is not contingent upon the approval of others. It will grow inside of you as you gain self-confidence in being yourself and being okay with yourself. The reason small children are incredibly authentic is because they have not yet experienced the monster of fear in their lives. They like themselves and expect everyone else to like them too. While we can't be that naïve as adults, we can practice authenticity by allowing ourselves to be genuine and sincere.

Self-authenticity is a discipline that must be practiced and grown as we develop the ability to trust ourselves.

The fourth step in the trust triangle is **conflict**. Through the years, it is amazing to me how many people see conflict as a negative thing. I've had leaders brag to me that their team never experiences conflict. I have listened as couples have told me that they never fight. In my opinion nothing could be more unhealthy.

Conflict is essential for people to feel safe expressing opinions that differ from the leader's opinion or their partner's opinion. Conflict is how new ideas are created, innovation is born, and critical thinking becomes most effective. Conflict simply means having a different opinion or idea from someone else. It does not have to be negative, violent or destructive.

Healthy conflict is what I'm speaking about. I believe it is absolutely necessary for any relationship or business to thrive. In order to develop the ability to personally understand conflict, you have to be willing to take a risk. Are you willing to confront someone in a healthy way, even when they do not respond in a healthy manner?

If you make your decision to confront based on someone's response, you are not engaging in personal healthy conflict. Put another way, we cannot depend on the response we get from someone else to motivate us to do the right thing. Having the fortitude and courage to display appropriate and healthy conflict to those around us is essential to building trust within ourselves.

We have to trust ourselves to not react when others aren't appropriate but to respond in a healthy way. Developing the self-discipline to handle conflict situations in a healthy manner takes much work. It is built on the previous trust step which is that we authentically want to do the right thing.

Developing an ability to have personal conflict in a positive way requires taking the time to learn what that actually looks like. Separating the person from the issue is where healthy conflict begins. Learning to have crucial conversations without personalizing is another key component. Realizing that conflict does not have to be win-lose but can be win-win is important. Many times, the goal is not to get someone to agree with you, but the goal is to be heard and to hear. Once that is accomplished, a compromise or an agreement to simply disagree can occur.

It is not the intent of this book to provide you with a detailed methodology for having healthy conflict. There are many resources available that will help you, should you want to grow your conflict

49

skills (I would recommend *Crucial Conversations* by Patterson, Grenny, McMillan, and Switzler as an excellent resource). The question that I ask you to answer is: are you willing to have healthy conflict even with those who do not respond in an appropriate manner? This is about how you respond not about how someone else responds.

At the pinnacle of the trust triangle is where **trust** is truly developed. It's where we strive to be. Trusting our self is not something that comes easily or with no work. It takes an intentional process, determination and a willingness to learn and grow on a personal level.

I believe learning to trust yourself may be the most important thing you can do to grow as a leader. It is also vital to have self-trust if you're going to have successful and vibrant relationships. Perhaps most importantly, developing self-trust will allow you to defeat the monster called fear.

No longer will you have to be afraid how you feel about yourself. You will not have to stay disconnected because you fear your feelings and emotions and where they will take you. Fear will no longer be able to negotiate with your non-negotiable values. You will no longer have to be afraid of conflict.

Choosing to grow your self-trust muscles can change your life. In order to begin the process, we must know where we stand currently with trusting ourselves. I challenge you to take a few minutes and complete the self-assessment below. Take time to think through each step of building self-trust. Don't rush through this short assessment but choose to start your journey toward self-trust by giving yourself permission to honestly answer the four questions below:

On a scale of 1 to 10 with one representing very little and 10 representing very much:

How well do you respect your self? _____ .

- Choosing to take of your body
- Choosing to draw boundaries in your life

How connected are you with your feelings and emotions?
_____

- Being self-aware of your feelings
- Emptying your emotional trashcan

How authentic are you on a daily basis? _____

- Knowing your non-negotiable values
- Owning your mistakes

How willing are you to engage in healthy conflict? _____

- Having the skills to confront without personalizing
- Realizing the importance of being heard and hearing

Total your score _____

If you scored 35-40, you have developed the skill of self-trust.
If you scored 30-34, you are well on your way to having self-trust.
If you scored 25-29, take the time to focus on your low score areas of self-trust.
If you scored below 25, now is the time to begin the journey of building trust in yourself.

This assessment is meant to be used as a tool to encourage you to continue your journey of building trust in yourself. Remember before you can really trust anyone else, you must first trust yourself.

Now let's take a look at the trust triangle as it applies to teams or organizations.

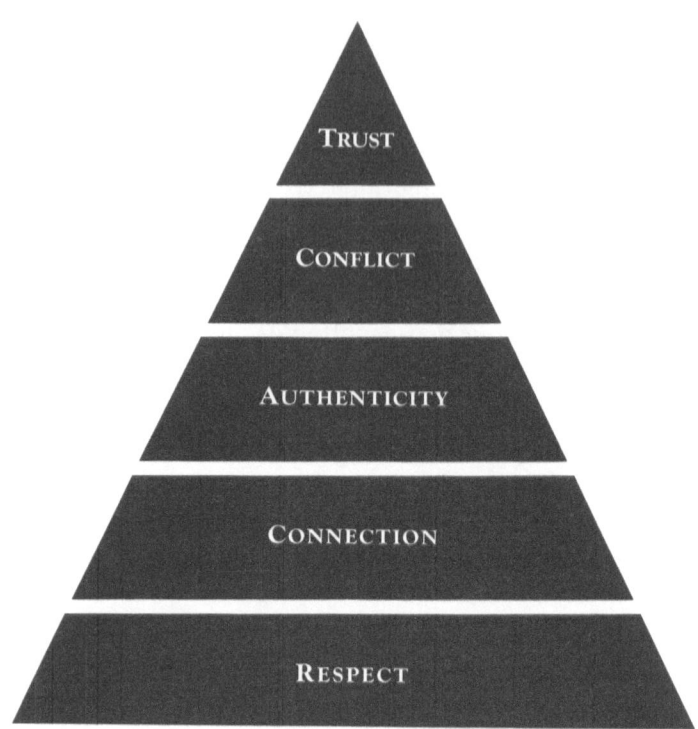

The Trust Triangle for Teams

Just as in building self-trust, a team that is centered around trust takes time, energy and effort. It is not a quick fix or a one-time event, it is a process.

The journey begins with respect. As we have previously discussed, respect is a choice. Choosing to respect the other members of your team simply because they are human beings is the cornerstone foundational piece to developing trust. That means honoring each person by allowing them to be heard and not judged. It means allowing each person to have a voice without being shut down. It does not mean agreeing or that the act of respect has been earned. In other words, you can have a lack of respect for someone's behavior while maintaining respect for that person as a human being. There must be the foundation of respect and how we treat one another if the team is to build trust. Foundational respect is not hierarchal, but it is distributed equally. This should be given the very moment a team is formed.

Developing connectivity on a team means choosing to engage in active listening and investing in each person individually within the team. Taking the time to learn about individual personalities, preferences and ways of thinking are what make teams connect. Team connection takes place above the line.

True connectivity occurs when team members work to understand and appreciate the differences found within the team. This means that team members must learn to speak the language of those who lead above the line as well as those who lead below the line. It is up to each individual to learn how to connect with her teammate.

Connection cannot take place when there is judgment, bitterness or resentment. It takes openness and appreciation in order for connectivity to grow. Also, it is important to remember that connectivity will not happen by osmosis. Simply being in the same room does not create connectivity.

Making the decision to be intentional about connecting with those on your team is the secret for success in this step of the trust triangle. Don't underestimate the importance of connecting. Without it, teams will experience silos, polarization and lack of productivity.

Developing authenticity within the team follows connection. Once you experience respect and connection, that gives the freedom for authenticity to occur. In fact, authenticity cannot occur until there is a true connection and respect found within the team. Authenticity within the team does not equal rudeness, arrogance, sarcasm or disrespect. It does mean that team members are free to express their personal views and they are appreciated for offering diverse thought and opinion.

Authenticity also requires team members to be able to own their mistakes. Creating a safe environment where a team member can raise their hand and say, "I blew this and I need help", is an essential key for success. This environment will not happen naturally and therefore it is important to be strategic and staging the environment that will lead the team to success.

By "staging environment" I mean setting appropriate boundaries guidelines and expectations for all team members from the very beginning. The team leader is responsible for creating an opportunity for authentic conversation to take place. The leader is responsible for making sure that team members are not judged or ridiculed for being different.

Teams that support and undergird authenticity develop a strong connection and respect for one another. As one component grows the others grow as well. Once a team experiences respect, connection and authenticity the culture is set for conflict.

As I discussed earlier, it is amazing how many teams are afraid of conflict. Many times they make it their goal not to have conflict and the result is detrimental for the team. Conflict is essential for a healthy team. Conflict is where voices of dissension can be heard in a safe place.

A team must learn to navigate dissenting opinions and disagreements among team members in a healthy way. If you do not have differing opinions and disagreements, you have a dictatorship that results in unilateral unhealthy thinking and decision-making. Show me a team that does not experience conflict and I will show you an unhealthy team. Either the team members are afraid to voice their opinion or they are apathetic about the team and its mission.

It is important to say here that while healthy conflict is vital inside the team meetings, it is deadly when taken outside the doors of the team meeting. There is no place for grumbling, complaining are sharing disagreements outside of the appropriate relationship or team. In other words, we are free to have a conflict behind closed doors, but we will not allow that to become toxic to our organization.

Healthy conflict must take place in the appropriate environment, with appropriate skill, and clear expectations of the result of the conflict. Healthy conflict should create a win-win result and not a win-lose result. That might mean that compromises are necessary. However, when mutual respect, connection, and authenticity are found within a team, compromise can be found as well.

So, the process goes as follows: the team begins with a foundation of mutual **respect** for one another. They understand that the cornerstone piece for a healthy successful team is their ability to offer respect to one another. When they establish the boundary of respect, they move to the next step toward trust which is connectivity.

Because there is respect, the team members are invested in one another. The **connection** is not just on a project or task level but on a personal level. They take the time to learn about their teammates' personality style. They learn to speak the language of the individual above or below the line.

As connection increases there comes a natural desire for and expectation of **authenticity.**

Team members now feel the freedom to express themselves without fear of being misunderstood or judged. Because there is a connection, there is an assurance that should a misunderstanding occur, it can be resolved more quickly as a result of the close connection of the team.

Authenticity allows for honest and deep conversation. It strengthens the team and allows expectations to be met without false pretense. The team now becomes ready to experience healthy **conflict**. This can be done because there is respect, connection and authenticity present within the team. Healthy conflict propels the team toward innovation, new ideas and effective and efficient productivity.

Once these components are present within a team, they can experience **trust.** This occurs between each member of the team and allows the team to perform at a much higher level. It also disarms the monster called fear. There is no fear of being disrespected, polarized, judged or being dictated to by a peer.

If you are a part of a team (this can be applied to personal and professional relationships as well), take a moment and complete the trust assessment tool below:

On a scale of 1 to 10 with one representing very little and 10 representing very much:

How well does the team demonstrate mutual respect toward one another? _____

- Choosing to honor other team members.
- Choosing to honor boundaries with one another.

How connected is the team with each other? _____

- Being aware of different personality types.
- Understanding and identifying below the line and above the line leadership styles.

How much does the team practice authenticity? _____

- The ability to have meaningful relevant conversations.
- The ability to raise your hand and say "I blew it" in a safe environment.

How well does the team engage in healthy conflict? _____

- Having the skills to confront without personalizing
- Realizing the importance of being heard and hearing

Total your score _____

If your team scored 35-40, they are operating with high trust.
If your team scored 30-34, they are well on their way to practicing trust.
If you your team scored 25-29, they should focus on the low areas and continue to build trust.
If your team scored below 25, now is the time to begin the journey of building trust as a team.

Because the process of building trust as a team or an individual takes time and hard work, many choose not to take the journey. We live in a society that loves instant gratification and quick fix remedies. But if we are going to address and defeat that monster called fear, we must commit ourselves to building trust. First, we must build trust within ourselves. We must learn to trust our responses, our intentions, our discipline and our behavior.

Once we have gained that self-trust and we are no longer victims of personal fear, we can focus on building trust in our teams and relationships. Choosing to begin the journey of trust can drastically improve your view of yourself and increase the depth and effectiveness of your relationship with others.

CHAPTER 6

Aligning the Process

In order to lead effectively above and below the line, there must be intentionality around developing a culture that supports this process. In other words, there must be alignment among the decision-makers of the organization in order for true change to take place. Keep in mind that the principles discussed are relevant for personal as well as professional relationships.

I know that the word "culture" has been overused in today's corporate and business communities. However, bear with me as I use this word to help us prepare to effectively lead above and below the line. For our purposes, culture is defined as "the behaviors and beliefs of an organization or relationship." Another way of defining culture is "having common beliefs and concerted actions and a collected pursuit of a clear result or purpose".

To be transparent, the above definitions come from my experience and research and therefore I'm sure I borrowed some of the definition from other sources. I use a simple formula call ABC's to help us practically apply these concepts. The equation is A + B = C, or

Action + Belief = Culture.

Action is found squarely below the line. However, without action there can be no culture of leading above and below the line. Action is where results are discovered. We must be committed to implement the plan or strategy otherwise there is no credibility in the process. Successful action includes rhythm and rigor and requires discipline.

Leaders who are action driven can create an environment of getting things done. This is not always a good thing. Creating mindless action leads to chaos. Getting things done if they are the wrong things or unnecessary things can prove detrimental to an organization.

While action is a critical component of a healthy culture, it alone will not suffice. While it may scratch an itch, the result of acting without purpose never works. It will inevitably cause obstacles and frustration for the team and organization. Nothing is more frustrating than to spend hours and hours working in the wrong direction.

Taking the time to create purposeful alignment with your team may be painful but it is important.

The next component of the equation is belief. This is found squarely above the line. Belief is determining the purpose and direction of the team or project. Do not assume that belief is a soft skill. It is not. In fact, it is a hard, sometimes difficult, skill to gain.

Creating belief means getting everyone aligned and pointed in the same direction with buy-in towards accomplishing the common goal or result. This is more than a patronizing agreement. It is taking the time to establish what the team believes should be accomplished and getting alignment around that goal.

This is an above the line process that requires discipline, rigor and rhythm. Notice that both above the line and below the line processes require these same leadership characteristics. Without discipline, rigor and rhythm there is no solid infrastructure in place in which to move forward.

Whether above or below the line, discipline is the characteristic needed to develop leadership muscle. It is what propels the leader to display strength and to "not be driven by emotion or feelings. Discipline requires IQ and EQ. It takes having the knowledge and skill to address the issue while possessing the ability to navigate yourself to accomplish the task.

Rigor is the depth of knowledge and a stern determination to dig deep and work hard. This is a characteristic that differentiates those who are committed to engaging in the process and those who are disengaged. Rigor is not a popular leadership topic, but it is absolutely essential to pursuing excellence above and below the line.

Rhythm comes from the Greek word "rhythmos" which means "measured motion". It is where patterns are developed, measured and adjusted. Without rhythm and metrics, there can be no reliable data or information. Rhythm builds sustainability in the process and is crucial in all areas of leading. Where there is no rhythm, there is no accountability.

Discipline, rigor and rhythm are necessary and key components for leading above and below the line.

Action + Belief = Culture. This simple equation can help your team to accomplish leading above and below the line with success. I recently encouraged a large organization which our company serves, to execute the concept of the ABC's and leading above and below the line. We designed rubber wrist bands with the equation written on them as a reminder to focus on a culture of leading at the next level. I love seeing the team members wearing them and effectively navigating above and below the line.

In a personal relationship, this formula works as well. If your actions in a relationship do not support what you say you believe about the relationship, then you have a toxic culture within that relationship. If you say one thing and do another you have an unhealthy relationship. Conversely, if your actions support what you said you believe about your relationship partner, then you are building a healthy culture in which the relationship can grow. This does not mean that you must always be perfect, however, you must be leaning into trying to grow the relationship.

Interestingly, the same characteristics of discipline, rigor and rhythm can be used in a personal relationship. It starts with being disciplined to make the other person a priority. The next step is to develop the rigor of investing in that person with your time, energy and effort. Finally, it is creating patterns of behavior that offer affirmation, love and security.

Let's answer five questions that will help us to develop the ability to effectively lead above and below the line. This process can be used at the beginning of any project, mission or objective. As you begin the process, answer the questions from the above the line perspective only. We will move to the below the line execution phase later.

1. **What is our purpose?**
   The temptation here is to answer this question below the line. For instance, we tend to say that our purpose is to accomplish the task at hand. Maybe we say that our purpose is to accomplish the goals set forth by the team or organization that we support. Perhaps your answer is that you are not sure of your purpose.

   It is important to think about your purpose from the above the line perspective. Your purpose as a leader is not simply to complete the task. It is much more than that. Your purpose may be to provide opportunities for those within your circle of influence. It could be to invest and develop other leaders around you.

   If you are a leader who dwells below the line and focuses on execution, you may be thinking that I have totally misunderstood your role within the organization. I challenge you to dare to think differently. Even with the below the line responsibility of execution, your purpose is not to simply be the expert that executes. At the minimum, it is to lead yourself well so that you might influence others in a positive way.

   Give this question serious thought on a personal and professional level.

   Challenge your team to wrestle with developing an above the line response to this question. Have a meaningful conversation with your relationship partner and discover each other's purpose as well as the purpose of your relationship.

It is a simple question with very complex and significant implications.

2. **What value do we provide?**
   What is your value? How do you measure it? What do you bring to the table? What is the value of your team? This is an important question to answer above the line in order to secure the relevance of your leadership. Remember the value we are speaking about here is not about tasking. It is not about getting the job done. It is about the value you provide above the line. It may be difficult for you to find value above the line. It will take discipline to allow yourself to create value in an area in which you may be uncomfortable.

   You may provide value by offering insight and wisdom for those you lead. Your value may be found in using the experience that you have gained in order to help the team navigate around potential pitfalls. You may have the ability to listen effectively and help your team members to process the mission and objective. You may have the ability to guide a team member to find a role in which he or she will be most effective. Your value may be found in empowering those around you to lead at the next level.

   I realize that most leaders who are used to finding value in their accomplishments find it very difficult to think about value above the line. This is especially true for those who are validated by accomplishing the task with excellence below the line. However, I challenge you to jump into the new and uncharted waters with self-trust and determination to grow your leadership skills. It will be a bit scary, but it will be rewarding.

   In a personal relationship, finding value may be harder than you think. Value that is above the line in a personal relationship means making that person better on a regular basis. Are you making the other person better or are you bringing him or her down? Adding value to the relationship means being intentional and requires selfless investment. When both people in a relationship add value, it is a healthy relationship.

3. **What are our habits?**

Once again, don't be tempted to answer this question below the line. I am not asking about the rhythms processes. This does not include actions and tasks that make up our daily execution routine. Think about good and bad habits we have with those around us. This includes how we communicate, polarize or isolate, encourage, deal with conflict or have hard conversations.

Maybe you have a habit of communicating every morning with your team. Maybe you have a habit of not dealing with difficult conversations that need to happen. You may have a habit of offering words of encouragement to your peers or those you lead. You may have a habit of using sarcasm as a form of communication. Your habit could be that you do not engage or talk to your peers on a regular basis.

Creating an honest list of habits will help us to continue the process of leading effectively above and below the line. As you think through this question make sure that you list your positive and negative habits. Work on self-awareness and the ability to see the truth in your patterns of behavior. We all have patterns that are good and patterns that are not so good. Choose to allow yourself to take a look at both.

On a personal level, discovering good and bad habits within the relationship is incredibly helpful. You may need to seek insight from your relationship partner in order to help you to identify some of the habits that you may not be aware. It could be that you have a habit of interrupting them when they are speaking. You could have the habit of offering positive affirmation on a regular basis. You may have a habit of being critical or negative. These are all important habits to recognize in the journey of creating a healthy relationship.

4. **What does success look like?**

   This is an incredibly important question, and it is almost always answered below the line. Let's take a different look at success. What does that success look like when it comes to our professional and personal relationships? How can we lead effectively if we do not know what we are moving toward as a leader? What does it mean to lead effectively above the line and how do we know when we get there?

   Success may not be something that is tangible. That does not mean that it is not valuable. It also does not mean that it cannot be defined. Success may look different above the line, but it is definitely something that is obtainable.

   Success may look like the team becoming more respectful of one another. It may look like having an authentic conversation with a peer. Success could be gained by consistent encouragement given from team members to their peers or those they lead. It could look like meaningful conversation or difficult conversations handled effectively. Success occurs when misunderstandings are cleared up quickly and efficiently. Success looks like loyalty spreading throughout the organization.

   You get the idea of what I am attempting to communicate. Take the time to redefine success above the line. Learn to think and appreciate new and different ways of successfully impacting others. Process how you can pursue excellence and success above the line.

   In a personal relationship, knowing what is healthy and what is toxic is critical. There is no perfect relationship, however relationships can be healthy and thus successful. What do you want out of your relationship? What would the relationship look like if you could script it to be anything you wanted it to be? What is it that your relationship partner wants out of the relationship? Take the time and identify what success looks like for your relationship.

5. **What are our priorities?**

Once you become aware of your habits and what success looks like, it's time to prioritize. What areas do we need to attack first? What areas are most important? This is an important exercise to create alignment within the team. It is where the rubber meets the road and priorities are set.

Think about the habits that you listed earlier. Which ones do you want to continue? Which ones do you want to improve on? Which ones do you want to eliminate? Now think about what success looks like. What actions do you need to take to accomplish success above the line?

Create an action item list of things you want to accomplish above the line. Be sure to include a timeline and the way to hold yourself or your team accountable for achieving these goals. Think of this as an above the line strategy plan. Create a structure that works for you and your team. The important thing is to make a tangible list that can be measured for accountability purposes. Because this is a below the line strategy plan, it will be easy to put it aside or not make it a priority. Do not give in to the temptation of minimizing the importance of your above the line strategy.

Prioritizing is also important in personal relationships. What are the major things that you need to work on in your personal relationships? Make sure that there is agreement on what to work on and what to wait on. When you invested the energy and time to create a priority list above the line for your relationships, you are sending a strong message that these relationships are important and you are willing to invest in them.

While the above five questions are useful in creating a strategy above the line, they can also be useful in creating a strategy below the line. Try using the questions on your next below the line project, allowing yourself to answer the questions below the line as needed.

Here is a structure that might be helpful in creating your action plan once you have answered the questions.

1. State the goal.
2. Develop the action items.
3. State the metrics.
4. What is the starting point?
5. What is the deadline for finishing?
6. Who is responsible for completing the action?
7. How will the action be measured?

The thought process of defining your purpose, identifying your value, looking at your habits, targeting success and then prioritizing action items is a sound methodology for creating a below the line execution strategy. I've seen it work in Fortune 100 corporations and in small businesses. Creating the structure and committing to the process generally yields a strong strategic plan that can be practically applied and implemented.

Once you have walked through these questions, you are ready to use the Crossing the Line equation for effective leading above and below the line:

Expectations + Priorities + Commitment = Focused Alignment

Goals + Data + Accountability = Measured Execution

This is the final part of the process that will yield tangible results for your team or relationship. Let's divert from the leadership process and take a look at the leader themself.

Leader versus Expert

I find that most leaders are validated from their knowledge, expertise or their occupation. I want to challenge you again to think differently. If you're going to lead more effectively and at a higher level, you must challenge yourself. In order to become a stronger leader, you must make the very difficult decision to no longer be the expert. There is a constant battle between wanting to lead and wanting to be the expert. Most leaders have found validation in becoming experts in their fields. Therefore, when challenged with leading instead of being the expert, there is usually hesitation and doubt.

However, if you are going to effectively lead others above or below the line you must increase your influence and credibility. You accomplish that by giving your credibility away. I know that sounds strange but stay with me. It's what leadership truly is about. You have to choose to move from being the expert to becoming the leader. The process is as follows:

You use your expertise to establish credibility. You then give the credibility to those on your team. Once there is focused alignment above the line you push that credibility and alignment under the line to measured execution. Once the execution process is in place, your role is to become the leader that provides above the line strategy for moving forward.

You move from being the expert below the line to establishing credibility and alignment for your team above the line. You then push alignment and execution below the line and then lead strategically above the line. Developing the ability to lead above and below the line is what great leadership looks like. This allows you as a leader to leap from building individual expertise and competency to creating greater organizational and team capacity.

If you struggle with having to be the expert here are four tips to help you leap into leadership above and below the line:

Leaping Tip 1: Build up your relationships.
This is the key to success for any leader. It also is one of the things that leaders struggle with the most. It is easy to get consumed with our day-to-day activities and responsibilities and neglect to invest the time it takes to build strong solid relationships. There is no question that leadership success centers on strong relationships. It's just difficult to justify

spending time developing these relationships if you are saturated with tasks and obligations below the line. Even those who dwell above the line can get caught up in philosophy and lose sight of actually making an effort to create strategic relationships. I can't over emphasize the importance of building relationships in your professional environment. They will make you or break you. Repeat after me.... relationships, relationships, relationships. Focus on them, improve them and create them.

Leaping Tip 2: Don't do the work—*enable* the work.
This will take a new mindset toward yourself and others. You cannot continue to do the work if you're going to grow your team and your organization. When we enable the work, we remove obstacles and create opportunities. It means that we realize that the work must be done, and we increase our capacity to accomplish the task by empowering and enabling others. This means that we must get out of their way. Nothing is more frustrating than asking someone to accomplish the task and then becoming an obstacle for him or her. If we are honest with ourselves, we might have to realize that doing the work is an ego builder for us. To move to the next level, we must check our ego and allow others to accomplish the task. This looks like allowing yourself to enable others to stretch their capabilities in new ways.

Leaping Tip 3: Don't have all of the facts but have an engaged presence.
Letting go and learning to trust your team is a key to taking the leadership leap. Being the expert, you were probably used to expecting and receiving the detailed data around a project or action item. You spent years learning to gather and interpret details and execute a plan of action. Allowing your team to gather facts and make decisions, including making mistakes, is crucial to your success as well as their success. Don't misinterpret this to suggest that you "check out". Quite the opposite. You must be engaged and able to lead without doing all of the fact-finding, data gathering work. You must

lead above and below the line through setting expectations with focused alignment and driving accountability with measured execution.

Leaping Tip 4: Get past the details and see the big picture. As a leader you must choose not to micromanage and to stay out of the details of the process. Your job is to keep your eyes on the big picture above and below the line. It is easy to lose sight of the 30,000-foot view when you are responsible for the execution and success of a task below the line. You find security in the details and safety in knowing exactly what is going on at all times. While this is how an expert operates, the need to micromanage will inhibit you from growing your leadership skills above and below the line. Don't give in to the temptation, instead, take the risk to lead differently. Big picture leading will take discipline, but it is the cornerstone to leaping to the next level.

In this chapter we have covered a lot of ground. We have talked about the ABCs of creating a leadership culture that included action and belief. We have challenged you to answer strategic leadership questions from an above the line point of view. We challenged you to become more than an expert and lead at a different level. Finally, we have given you tips for leaping from being an individual contributor to increasing the team and organizational capacity.

I hope that this chapter has caused you to pause and think about your professional life as well as your personal life. I hope that you gave serious consideration to the culture that you are leading and creating both at home and in your work environment. Being honest with yourself about your actions and beliefs and whether or not they align can be insightful and hurtful. If you identify areas of action that you need to change ... congratulations! Thank you for being authentic and open to learn and grow as a leader.

Please know that no leader has all of the answers or is perfect. We all struggle with creating a healthy culture for those we lead as well as those we care about. It is a difficult challenge to learn to lead above and below the line. I hope that this chapter has provided somewhat of a structure for you to process your personal and professional relationships. I truly believe that the concepts in this chapter can help change your leadership style in a positive way.

I get excited when I see leaders who are willing to take the risk of crossing into unknown, and at times difficult, waters of growth. Trying to lead in an area that is foreign to you can be intimidating and frustrating. Not knowing exactly what leading at the next level looks like or what it means to lead above the line or navigate below the line can be excruciatingly painful. However, when a leader chooses to risk their comfort and security in order to discover new territories of leadership, it is incredibly exciting. Furthermore, watching these leaders grow as men and women who understand the importance of leading above and below the line is very inspiring.

I hope that you're considering moving from being the expert to becoming the leader. As you think about and process your next steps, I hope they include letting go of the security of being the expert and taking on the honor of leading and influencing others.

I recently led a group of highly technical executives who worked for a mega corporation through the above the line process. It was intriguing to see the brilliant minds in the room and how they authentically struggled with learning to lead above as well as below the line. There was debate, disagreement and genuine conversation around how we can improve our leadership.

In their high demand jobs where execution and productivity are the name of the game, they could've chosen to invalidate the whole process and focus on the many responsibilities and demands that were pounding on them every day. Instead, they chose to do what great leaders do. They opened their minds and hearts to learn how to better lead the people who have been entrusted to their supervision and leadership.

We ended the day with an action plan and commitments that would be very difficult to implement and sustain. Yet these strong leaders were not afraid to take the risk to invest in a leadership philosophy in which they were uncomfortable but committed. They realized that the people they lead were more important than the processes that were in place. However, they also realized that the processes were the reason that the people were able to successfully do their jobs. Finding this balance between tasks and people was agonizing at times. These executives had the responsibility of leading literally thousands of individuals. These courageous leaders committed to take the time to invest in the personal lives of their teams. They realized that building connection was essential to the success of their teams. They wanted to get this leadership thing right and were willing to cross the line to do so.

As we walk through the process of crossing the line and learning to give credibility away through focused alignment and measured execution, I could see the determination in their faces. They said, "We do not want to be just another group of executives who become victim to the demands of output goals and objectives." I would be untruthful unless I told you that this is still a huge dilemma in this organization. There are leaders who realize the need for change and there are leaders who are determined to stay in their comfort zone and take no risks.

What I really admire about this group of leaders is that they were willing to go against the norm of corporate leadership and explore, ... no... pioneer, new opportunities. It takes courage to forge into unknown territories of leadership. It takes bravery to take the risks that will force you to think and behave differently. However, when you are committed to becoming a person of influence and you understand the power of influence, it is worth the risk.

I have walked with this group for several years and have seen their highs and lows. I've watched as they struggle to meet corporate demand and still maintain the integrity of a leader who cares about her people. Leadership is messy. It is not easy and it is not simple. By the way, all of these executives at one time were considered an expert in his or her field. Each one has made the commitment to give away their credibility in order to lead above and below the line. It has been

Dr. Larry Little

fun to see the culture of their teams and divisions change as they lead differently. I continue to learn from these highly intelligent men and women who understand the value of influence.

One of the executives, who may be one of the brightest men I've ever met, taught me a very valuable lesson. We have walked together for several years and I have observed how this corporation leans on him when a highly technical problem arises. Time after time he has risen to the occasion.

We were discussing the concept of leading others well above and below the line when he made a statement that I think of and use often. He said:

"Never mistake brilliance for direction and purpose."

People need your direction and purpose more than your brilliance.

CHAPTER 7

EQ or IQ?

I have a question for you. Which is more important, IQ or EQ? IQ is a measurement of cognitive intelligence, and EQ is the measurement of emotional intelligence. Which do you believe is more important?

For years, the science of emotional intelligence (EQ) was not given much credibility in the business realm. It was discounted as being irrelevant for execution and accomplishing tasks, and inconsequential to the bottom-line results of an organization. While that faulty thinking has been proven to be lacking, there are still those who believe that EQ has no place in the business world. In other words, it's fine to talk about emotional intelligence at home or in our families, but it is of no importance in the work environment.

It is curious to me how this 1950s philosophy of leading still exists in pockets of outdated companies and organizations. Despite a plethora of research and publications on the topic, many leaders still downplay emotional intelligence as being an irrelevant "soft skill" that is too touchy-feely to have merit in the data-driven world of business. The importance of leading above the line and facilitating self-awareness and trust takes a back seat to intelligence and technical capability.

In a 2015 article written by the Harvard School of Professional Development, Professor Laura Wilcox states that "emotional intelligence accounts for nearly 90% of what moves people up the ladder in the organization, when IQ and technical skills are roughly similar." If this is true, then why do so many business leaders discount the importance of EQ and shy away from Above the Line leadership tactics? She goes on to explain that there are two parts of our brain that are vying for control. One is the neocortex which holds the cognitive neurotransmitter network—the home of IQ. The other is the amygdala, which controls the emotional network of the brain—where EQ resides. Interestingly, the neocortex can process a factorial of four variables with just 24 possible interrelationships. The amygdala, on the other hand, can process 100 times faster than the neocortex. (2019, Emotional Intelligence Is No Soft Skill, President and Fellows of Harvard College)

This can be a good or a bad thing. When our EQ highjacks our IQ we make bad decisions based on feelings and emotions. This takeover is what has given EQ a bad reputation in the work environment. When leaders respond out of pure emotion and without any data-based reasoning, they rarely make good decisions. It is for this reason that many leaders refuse to travel above the line in their leadership—they are afraid of being hijacked by emotions.

However, we know that being able to effectively lead above and below the line, using IQ and EQ in concert, is a strong differentiator that offers any organization a competitive advantage. The leader who understands how to effectively wield IQ and EQ can inspire their teams to increase employee engagement and raise the team morale, ultimately leading to increased productivity and better company-wide results. Without EQ, teams and organizations will fail to ever develop the kind of cohesion, trust, and team dynamics that are critical for an organization to thrive. EQ is a critical component not only of creating a strong company culture, but of the overall success and bottom-line growth of a company.

The Case for EQ

Over and over again as I've asked leaders to describe the greatest challenges that they face within their organizations, the number one answer is communication. They struggle to communicate with their teams, their peers and their bosses. Expectations are not expressed in an effective way, conflict is not handled appropriately, and the ability to motivate employees is a constant struggle. Likewise, the ability to assess and evaluate the effectiveness of products, processes and procedures is based on clarity of communication. All of these issues are addressed from above the line.

That is why executives and recruiters in today's business communities are seeking to recruit those who have the ability to display and develop EQ. I can personally attest to the fact that when employees are hired with the relative same level of IQ, EQ can make a huge difference in increasing the success of the employee, along with the contribution that the person can make to the organization.

It is tempting for leaders to rely on the intelligence and technical skills of their team members to help them succeed. Particularly in Science, Technology, Engineering and Math (STEM) based industries, I have encountered business leaders who are perplexed when they promote their most brilliant and technically competent employees into the role of a manager or team leader, and then that individual and their team begin to flounder and performance plummets. Shouldn't someone who is great at their job be able to lead others to be equally great in their contributions?

In fact, I would argue that the companies who hire the most intelligent people in the world are the companies who most need to prioritize developing EQ and the ability to cross the line with their leaders. Our company, Eagle Center for Leadership, works with a large, highly technical Aerospace engineering organization. They have a reputation for being able to provide solutions and products that address difficult and highly technical needs both domestically and internationally. They are one of the fastest growing aerospace companies in the world, and they are able to recruit the brightest and the best.

I recently asked Dave King, the current President of this organization, the same question that I asked you. Which is more important when hiring, IQ or EQ? His answer hints at the success of his organization. He said, "We know that we can find brilliant men and women to hire. What we look for once we have established a baseline IQ and technical skill is someone who has the capacity and willingness to develop EQ." He continued, "In the highly competitive market that we serve, understanding and possessing EQ is a definite advantage, both internally and externally".

I have watched Dave lead for several years. I have observed his unique ability to hire executives that possess the EQ needed to cross the line between focused alignment and measured execution. He possesses an enormous amount of EQ and IQ himself, and he has seen firsthand how important both are to the success of a leader and an organization.

You see, Dave's company has always been strong in the measured execution arena. Their processes, data collection and accountability metrics are where they are naturally most comfortable. However, despite their highly intelligent work force, years ago it became evident that there were gaps in their organization that were hindering their success. They found that their growth was being threatened by linear thinking and an aversion to change.

The leaders of the company decided to create a culture of Crossing the Line. They chose to invest in their team's leadership skills by developing the EQ of their engineer-heavy employee base. They offered relationship classes, effective communication seminars and coaching on how to build strong relationships. They also held their leaders accountable to growing and developing relationships with their peers, their teams and even the C-suite executives. This skill also helped them to become very effective at building relationships with new and existing customers. The company created focused alignment by developing expectations, priorities and getting commitments from their teams—all work that was done above the line.

Once they began developing the EQ of their very bright work force and using those EQ skills to implement using Crossing the Line concepts, they saw their gaps diminish and momentum soar. This company continues to educate and coach employees in using the Crossing the Line techniques. They encourage their employees not just to lead in the office but to cross the line with their families and in their personal relationships.

They have been on an incredible growth curve and have seen unprecedented success in the last several years, and they continue to be committed to developing not just the technical skills of their team, but the interpersonal leadership skills—the EQ—that really makes a difference.

Winning Hearts and Minds

It is important to know that people above the line and below the line follow leaders who have the ability to win their hearts and minds. The Business Journal published an article on January 8, 2009 citing a study entitled "What Followers Want From Leaders" by Rath, Conchie and Gallup. This study involved a research team which asked more than 10,000 followers what the most influential leaders contributed to their lives. The answers were trust, compassion, stability and hope. All are squarely above the line.

Before you write this study off as being irrelevant, think about how each of these characteristics are vital for the success of any team, organization or relationship. Effective leaders must gain the trust of their team if they expect them to listen to their guidance. They must show compassion when teaching their team how to learn from their mistakes. The leader must demonstrate stability in order to effectively lead through a time of crisis. They must offer the hope that a job well done will come with recognition and reward.

Those who are more comfortable below the line may think that they cannot win the hearts and minds of their team because they are not articulate or charismatic. I once worked with a leader whose personality make-up was most comfortable residing squarely below the line. However, of all the leaders I had worked with, this particular leader had the ability to capture the hearts and minds of his followers in a way that I had never experienced. In the Make A Difference vernacular he was a Leading Lion/Competent Camel. I spent years walking with him and learning from him. He led literally thousands of people and effectively gained the trust and loyalty of each of them.

So, what set this below the line leader apart? I believe it began with his humility and ended with his strength. Although he was incredibly task-driven, he was able to pull others around him who had greater people-skills than he did. He allowed his team to use their strengths above and below the line. Furthermore, he was an incredible listener and demonstrated a genuine respect for all those he led and with whom he worked. However, when hard decisions had to be made, he was on the forefront of making the call and taking responsibility for failures while giving others credit for success.

My relationship with this leader continues to this day and he continues to win the hearts and minds of those within his circle of influence. He is a great reminder that strong leadership is a choice, and it can happen below or above the line.

You see, gaining trust with your team is not about charisma or eloquent speech. Trust is a result of consistently showing authentic care and concern for other people. This includes the ability to confront when necessary and encourage when needed. It is a learned behavior that the below the line leader can practice and hone.

In any competitive sport, a person or team must endure long hours of practice and discipline if they're going to be successful at game time. It would be foolish for a team to enter a competition with no preparation and expect to be successful. Likewise, in order to win the hearts and minds of your team, a below the line leader must commit to prepare themselves for leading in a way that will be uncomfortable at times. They must commit to learn a new discipline.

Let me clarify that I am not advocating for the below the line leader to change who they are. I am challenging them to lead at a different level. This means understanding the importance of trust, compassion, stability and hope in developing strong teams. It may mean working hard to provide resources and tools aimed at above the line concepts. It also could mean learning how to leverage above the line leaders around you to help accomplish your mission.

How Do You Make Them Feel?

Maya Angelou once remarked,

> *"People will forget what you said, people will forget what you did, but people will never forget how you made them feel."*

Think about someone who has had a negative impact on your life—someone who did not make you feel good, and likely made you feel quite bad about yourself or a situation. Their influence has caused you to be frustrated, disappointed or discouraged. Whenever you think of this person you know that they are not who you want to follow or how you want to model your leadership. For some this is a very difficult exercise and brings back deep hurt or pain. The memory serves as a reminder of how not to treat others and how not to use your influence.

Now think about someone who makes you feel good and valued, someone who has had a positive impact in your life. Their influence has inspired you to be better, stronger and to strive to meet your full potential as a person or leader. You have learned life lessons from this person. You have watched as they used their influence to speak into the lives of others. When you think of this person it brings encouragement to your heart and serves as a motivator to you.

We all have positive and negative influences in our lives. Unfortunately, part of living means walking through the valley of difficult relationships. It includes, for many, being exposed to those who have hurt us or led us down an unhealthy path that had destructive consequences. It also includes those who have lifted us, inspired us and encouraged us. For some it has literally changed the course of their lives.

I strongly believe that we choose how we influence. This above the line skill begins with leading ourselves well. The first person we must influence is our self. This means being intentional about how we behave and being aware of the choices that we make every day. As influencers we do not have the right to negatively impact those within our personal or professional communities. Taking personal responsibility is where EQ and influence begin. It is the foundational characteristic for any successful leader on any level.

CHAPTER 8

You Gotta Have It: GRIT

The question is, how do we become leaders; men and women, of positive influence? If we are going to make a commitment to becoming leaders who positively influence the lives of others on a personal and professional level, it requires something I call GRIT.

G- GET OVER YOURSELF

The first letter of our GRIT acronym, G, reminds us that in order to be a truly great leader you've got to GET OVER YOURSELF. It might sound harsh, but the root of effective leadership lies in a willingness to put your own needs and wants aside and prioritize the growth and success of other people. This requires a healthy dose of humility, and humility is something that can be harder and harder to hold on to, the further we progress in our careers and the more important sounding our title becomes.

I will never forget the time I spent with a particular CEO of a large international corporation. From the moment I met him, it was obvious that he was interested in one person, and one person only—himself. I remember talking with him about a team member of his that I was coaching. He could only say negative things about this person. His constant looking at his watch and over my shoulder told me he was not truly engaged in this conversation or invested in helping his team member to grow and succeed. His arrogance created a negative atmosphere for everyone around him. He is no longer the CEO, but I have to wonder how his legacy of leading will be interpreted throughout the organization and beyond.

Most people acknowledge that self-centered leaders are largely ineffective leaders. And yet, I believe that arrogance and self-importance is one of the greatest pitfalls that trap leaders. In fact, most leaders who refuse to cross the line do so not because they don't know how to or are incapable of developing the skills that they need to lead others well—it is because of their own arrogance.

Take the below the line leader, for example. They know that putting themselves out of their comfort zone and working on things like culture and leadership philosophies will be incredibly uncomfortable and require them to be more vulnerable than they're used to being. They'll have to acknowledge that leading above the line isn't their strength and be willing to do it anyway. This is incredibly uncomfortable for a below the line leader, and therefore they might decide to stay right where they are, safely below the line. While they may stay comfortable, this kind of selfish leadership that prioritizes their own desires over the needs of their team will never inspire others to follow them.

Conversely, the above the line leader may allow their arrogance to make them equally unwilling to lead below the line. This leader is more comfortable staying safely in the realms of inspiring words and big ideas, but when it's time to develop the discipline necessary to follow through on the words and execute on those ideas, the arrogant above the line leader shies away from the intense work and effort it would require them to learn to move and lead below the line. When this leader decides to prioritize their own comfort and stay above the line where they feel safe and in charge, their inability to get over themselves and get where their team is will result in a lack of action and results that will destroy their credibility as a leader and demoralize their team.

We can see that above and below the line leaders both run the risk of letting their own arrogance and selfishness get in the way of their success as a leader. This is why it is critical that we constantly remind ourselves of the need to get over ourselves and begin to understand the minds and hearts of those that we are leading. This endeavor to understand others and get where they are is what we call empathy.

Get Over Yourself- Practicing Empathy

The first thing to understand about empathy is that it is not a feeling, but rather a choice. We do not *feel* empathy for others, we *choose* to have empathy for others. It is active and actionable, and a skill that can be practiced and developed through rigor and rhythms of choosing empathy again and again as we seek to better understand and lead those around us day by day and moment by moment.

Empathy is often misunderstood as being "soft" or seen as a weakness. This couldn't be further from the truth. In fact, empathy requires a type of bravery that only the most courageous can achieve—the bravery of vulnerability. It is much easier for us to make decisions from our own prejudices, opinions, and views of the world. Empathy requires us to let down our barriers, engage in meaningful conversations, and switch out the lenses with which we've become used to viewing life through in order to authentically attempt to understand the viewpoints, pain, goals, and motivators of someone else, possibly even someone very different than us.

When we practice empathy, we allow our own perception and ideas to be challenged by taking an honest look at how someone else's views might compliment or contradict our own. This is why empathy is not for the faint-hearted; it requires the kind of bravery that comes from being secure enough in who you are that you aren't threatened by who other people choose to be. I believe that leaders who are unwilling or unable to listen to and understand the viewpoints of others are acting out of fear and insecurity.

Empathy doesn't mean changing your mind or your beliefs, it simply means being willing to listen with an open mind and seek to understand. The leader who has the courage to have meaningful conversations with those who differ from her is the leader who will consistently make better decisions. There are times when developing an understanding of those who differ from you will change your thought process. There are other times when it will not. Either way, you will come away from an experience of true empathy as a stronger leader than you were going into it. So, you see, empathy not only shows those around us that we care about them and value them, it also helps us grow into better leaders ourselves.

If we want to be great leaders, then we must practice empathy not only with those we lead at work, but with those we live with and love at home, as well. We can demonstrate empathy to those with whom we have personal relationships, by being careful not to judge but to show understanding. Even when, perhaps especially when, we do not agree with our relationship partner, we still do not have to judge. We can show understanding and still agree to disagree. Empathy is about having an attitude of acceptance and understanding. Fighting to get our opinion across or trying to win an argument will create an environment of hostility and distrust. Showing empathy looks like taking the time to fully understand before offering an opinion. It is allowing your loving concern for the other person to override your temptation to judge. Showing empathy is being understanding when your relationship partner has interests and obligations that do not include you. Instead of demonstrating jealously or insecurity, show empathy by encouraging and supporting him or her. Remember, empathy is not a feeling, it is an action.

Get Over Yourself- Own Your Failures

Of course, the most difficult times for us to Get Over Ourselves and practice humility is when we really make a mess of things and have to own up to our mistakes and failures. As a leader, you will never earn the respect of those you lead until you can learn to take responsibility and own the failure when you blow it. And believe me, you will blow it, in big ways and small, throughout your leadership journey and life. The key to success is not avoiding failure, but owning it, learning from it, and moving forward better because of it.

I was recently having a conversation with my wife of 36 years, who is a Competent Camel in our Make A Difference vernacular. This particular conversation was taking place over a quick dinner after I'd gotten home from a day at work, and I was half-heartedly engaging with her while watching some game or another on the television over her shoulder. In true Competent Camel fashion, she was going over the tiny details of a project at our house that I wasn't particularly invested in, and after a few minutes of her interrupting my attention on my game to ask me detailed questions and request equally detailed responses, I snapped at her. I'm not proud of it, but my tone got angry and my words were sharp, and I immediately knew that I had overreacted. It was totally inappropriate and over the line, and not at all what the loving woman who so carefully tends to the needs of our home deserves from me. "Honey, I'm sorry. That was way out of line, and you did nothing wrong. That one was on me entirely. I'm going to turn the TV off now and give you my full attention." She looked and me and seeing that I was sincere, responded graciously and we let the whole incident go and moved on with our evening.

Now, I'd like to tell you that I always handle my mistakes that quickly and seamlessly. However, the truth is that after 36 years of marriage there have been many blow ups and overreactions on my end, and the worst results were when I would choose to sulk or storm off or blame someone else after I knew I'd made a mistake. Over the years, I've learned that our relationship is better when I build trust with my wife through owning my mistakes, and the sooner the better. The same principle holds true with the people you lead and work with professionally. The sooner you are able to own it when you inevitably mess up, the sooner you can get back on track with a team that trusts you and is willing to work together to achieve your shared goals.

It helps to remember the principle that people will follow those that they like. Nothing makes a person more approachable and likable than when they admit their flaws and mistakes and own up to their failures. Our failures present us with the opportunity to connect with those around us by showing our vulnerability. People connect with others much more over their failures and flaws than their successes and achievements, and nothing is more humanizing than someone admitting to their mistakes and authentically endeavoring to grow from them.

A wise leader that I work with once shared a saying that I've never forgotten—*"Failure doesn't have to be fatal."* If we are willing to get over ourselves and own our failures, they will not kill us, but will instead make us stronger, more trustworthy leaders.

Get Over Yourself- Choosing Humility Over Arrogance

If we are to Get Over Ourselves and lead others well, we must choose to be intentional about practicing empathy, owning our mistakes, and developing humility every single day. It is critical to remember that none of these things are feelings or character traits, but rather they are choices that must be made and skills that can be developed with practice. There are no excuses, only choices.

At the end of the day, the only excuse we have for not choosing to Get Over Yourself is selfishness and arrogance. If you believe that you are better than the people around you, that you are above making and owning your mistakes, or that your title or position protects you from needing to understand others around you, then you will never be a great leader. This kind of thinking is delusional and based in narcissism, but unfortunately, it's found in many leaders—I'd bet that you could name a few right now.

The good news is that this kind of thinking can be changed, and the first step is choosing to practice humility and Get Over Yourself.

R- RUN TO THE HARD THINGS

The second component to being a leader with GRIT is that you must learn to Run To The Hard Things. This notion is so contradictory to our modern society's values of ease and convenience that it almost sounds crazy. Who wants to run TOWARDS hard things? Haven't we spent our lives trying to create efficiencies and automations to make our lives easier? We can order groceries and have them delivered to our door two hours later. We have apps that let us start our cars before we even get to the parking lot. Our music can be turned on and tuned to our favorite playlists with voice command, without us ever needing to lift a finger. We're all constantly trying to answer the question, "How can I make my life easier?"

Contrary to what society and those profiting off of all these conveniences might have us believe, I have found that it's the leaders that choose to not only *do*, but to *embrace* doing hard things that truly excel and achieve greatness. Think of an athlete for example—do you think there is a single Olympic medalist in any sport that didn't spend hours of every day for years, likely decades, in training, putting their body through incredibly difficult and painful exercises and conditioning practices, depriving themselves of sleep and disciplining themselves to stick to the most rigorous levels of nutrition and wellness? I doubt there's ever been a single Olympic athlete, much less gold medalist, who slept in, spent their time playing video games and avoiding physical training, and ate junk food. Although that would have been easier, it would never have gotten them a gold medal.

Similar to an athlete, great leadership is something that you can train for and improve with hard work, rigor, and discipline. It will require sacrifice and pain and effort, but the reward is great. We can only get there if we choose to not walk but *run* towards the hard things. I realize that this is not always our natural tendency, however.

A friend of mine shared a story with me about the cows and the buffalo that live in Colorado. He said that in a specific part of the state, there are vast plains filled mostly with herds of cows, and the occasional herd of buffalo. Every now and then a big storm will blow in, and typically these storms form in the west and move towards the east. As the storm begins brewing overhead, the cows will notice the shift in the weather and, wanting to avoid the storm, they will begin running east, trying to outrun the storm forming in the west. The problem with this tactic is that cows are not very fast runners. If you've ever seen a cow run, you can attest to the fact that these bovines are not likely to outrun a storm. In fact, the storm generally overtakes the cows as they're running, and the animals find themselves running with the storm and getting even more battered by it than if they had just stayed where they were.

Buffalo, on the other hand, seem to have developed a more effective tactic. When they see a storm brewing in the west, they do the exact opposite of our cow herd; they run west, directly towards the storm. In doing so, they actually run through the storm, usually before it gets bad, and spend less time in the storm than do the cows that ran away from it.

You see, the buffalo have learned the lesson of running *toward* the hard things.

To be honest I have no idea if this is true, or just a powerful story that my friend shared with me, but there is certainly truth in the illustration. When we behave like cows and run away from the hard things, many times we find ourselves in worse shape than if we had simply addressed the same problem head-on. When our tendency is to run instead of to confront and we refuse to face the hard things in life, we weaken our leadership muscles and waste our energy.

I'd like to share a story with you about what running towards hard things can look like for a leader in their workplace. There's a leader who I've walked with for several years, and I have learned a lot from his life and leadership. His name is Phil Marshall. When he took a new position as an executive at a large manufacturing company several years ago, Phil started a practice that at the time, was difficult for him. He began the process and ritual of intentionally walking the aisle of the manufacturing line every day. He told me that although he is an introvert and would typically prefer to stay in his office, he wanted to earn the right to lead at this new organization, and he knew that would require him to form relationships with his new team members.

For the first several months of his new job, he spent a significant amount of time every single day walking the floor, asking questions and allowing the team members on the floor to teach him about their responsibilities and tasks. Phil not only learned what each employee was responsible for doing and how their role contributed to the organization, but he also sought to develop a personal relationship with each of his new team members. He asked all kinds of questions and made it a point to learn as much about his employees personally as he could. He learned about their families, their interests, their goals, and their favorite sports teams. He learned who they were as people, as well as employees of his new organization.

This commitment to spend time on the floor and get to know his team put Phil out of his comfort zone and pushed him to practice crossing above and below the line as needed as he got to know each team member in different capacities. Soon, instead of dreading when the boss came around, the employees and stakeholders that worked on his team began to look forward to his daily walk of connection. He treated the front-line team members with respect and consequently, he garnered their respect. Instead of shying away from getting to know the new team, he faced the challenge head on and went to where his team was to do the work of forming intentional relationships. He ran towards the hard thing, and it paid off.

He still makes time to walk through the plant on a regular basis. His down-to-earth, authentic style of leading has propelled him to be incredibly effective and highly trusted among the team. Today, his team is performing at a higher level than ever before, and they have a leader that they respect and trust, cheering them on.

While Phil's commitment to forming relationships is an excellent example of running towards the hard things above the line, we must also be willing to run towards the hard things below the line when called upon to do so. This means tackling the disciplines and tasks that are essential to running a successful organization. This may look like creating and running systems and processes that serve as the infrastructure for the company or it may look like digging into a technology that requires incredible focus and expertise. It could look like creating and running a manufacturing process that allows the plant to perform at a higher level. In other words, running toward the hard thing must include accountability and sustainability.

Think about the hard things in your life. Maybe there is a personal conversation you need to have with someone you love. Maybe you need to address an issue that has been the elephant in the room for a long time. Perhaps you need to make a decision that you have been putting off but you know it is the right thing to do. Maybe there's something you need to stop doing. Maybe there is something you need to start doing. Learning to run toward the hard thing is choosing to not allow fear to drive us toward the path of least resistance. It is choosing not to put our head in the sand when difficult opportunities present themselves to us.

Choosing to run toward those things while being uncomfortable is definitely the stuff of strong leaders. It is scary to run into a storm. Facing the clouds of fear and insecurity or running headlong into the thick of conflict is incredibly difficult. Taking on the challenge that no one else wants to address can be very intimidating. Developing the ability to run to the hard thing is not a soft or pleasant leadership skill. However, it is essential if we are going to continue to grow as leaders. Commit to being a buffalo and running towards the hard things in your life, and watch your leadership strengthen.

I- INSPIRE OTHERS

We know that we need to Get Over Ourselves. We understand that we must choose to Run Towards the Hard Things. The next thing that we must do in order to be a leader with GRIT is Inspire Others. Now, before you "check out" because you're not that kind of "rah rah, go team go" inspirational leader, hear me out—inspiration is rarely about what you say or how you say it. Inspiration does not require charisma or an eloquent way of speaking. You don't need to deliver heart-felt speeches to cheering crowds or create memorable mnemonic messages to spread throughout your company in order to be an inspirational leader. I believe that we are most inspired by others not because of what they say, but because of what they do. So, the question becomes not, "What can I *say* to inspire my team?", but rather, "What can I *do* to inspire them?".

The word "inspire" comes from a Latin word *inspirare,* meaning "to breathe or blow into". For me this brings to mind the act of blowing on a spark to help it grow into a flame. When we inspire others, what we're really doing is breathing life over their spark and encouraging it to grow into a flame. It is not fanning your own flame. It is doing something for someone else and giving of yourself with no agenda or expectations in return. Inspiration is not about impressing others with our words or acts of valor, but rather the ability to recognize something good and valuable in someone else and help them strengthen that trait and grow as a person.

Inspiration is a behavior. You behave your way to inspiring others. Inspiration is felt from how we act and how we treat others on a daily basis. It is how we choose to use our words, and more importantly it is the actions that surround those words. There are a few actions that I recommend you make a habit of, if you strive to inspire those around you, and I'll go through them in the next few sections.

Inspire Others- Be A Servant

The generation that we call "Millennials" has been creating problems for the traditional work force ever since they began to enter it. Leaders know that these young team members have a lot of creativity and a valuable perspective to offer but have struggled to tap into their energy and understand how to motivate, incentivize, and inspire these non-conforming idealists. According to a *Forbes* article by Jenna Goudreau, Millennials place a higher priority on giving back and serving others than did previous generations. "A comprehensive study by the Pew Research Center found that millennials place a higher priority on helping people in need (21%) than having a high-paying career (15%)." These young people would rather give to those in need than earn more money—now that is inspiring!

In this instance, the Millennial generation has it right. Inspiring others begins with a servant leader's heart. Above the line, this means being willing to speak into the lives of those you are leading. It means putting others before yourself. It means being intentional about developing and growing those around you to become the leaders that they want to be.

Remember though, servant leadership is not an attribute, it is an action. It must exist above the line as an ideal or value, but below the line is where the work of servant leadership really takes place. Below the line, the servant leader puts their money, time, and effort where their mouth is and takes action to give to and invest in others. Servant leadership is made more effective when we create and maintain systems and processes that enable others to succeed and grow. This means creating tangible relevant metrics and dashboards that inspire team members to work together. Feedback metrics are most effective when they are inspiring. If the feedback is not accurate or is too ambiguous, it can have the opposite effect. Accurate feedback inspires below the line teams to improve, sustain, or change directions. It serves as a compass or map for executing on goals by serving one another and working together. This must be encouraged and facilitated by the leader.

Perhaps the most important place that most of us can practice giving and serving is in our personal relationships. Serving those we love is a display of humility that says to them, "You are important to me." The first step is to develop an attitude of servant leadership. It is putting our own desires aside and focusing on meeting their needs. We must become invested and focused on helping them to grow in the ways that are important to them. Inspirational serving can occur above or below the line. Above the line it may look like words of encouragement or having conversations that are important to them. Below the line it might look like taking time to do the things that they enjoy like hiking, biking, watching movies (you get the idea). It may also look like joining them and accomplishing tasks that are important to them like remodeling a room, parenting, gardening (again, you get the idea).

Inspire Others- Gratitude

Another key component to inspiring others is showing gratitude as a leader. Having the humility to show thankfulness to those around you has many benefits. An executive with many years of leadership experience asked me a question that I simply cannot get off my mind. He asked, "Do you think most people would rather have someone help them with a task or would they rather hear a 'thank you' from someone they have helped?" Your first impulse might be that someone would much prefer "help with the task." However, after much reflection on this question, I wonder if that is true? A "thank you" is often a symbol that lets us know that we have been seen and heard, and that our efforts, time and energy on behalf of someone else have been acknowledged and appreciated.

There is power in acknowledging and appreciating the effort and skills of others. It not only shows respect, but it gives a wonderful gift to those who have helped us—the gift of gratitude.

Practicing gratitude may be as simple as saying "thank you" more often. Showing appreciation is contagious and when you lead from a gracious spirit your team will catch that mindset. By demonstrating to those around you how to give and receive graciously, you set the tone for inspiring leadership. The ways that we can show gratitude to those around us are limitless, and gratitude can be expressed above the line in words and acknowledgement and below the line with feedback mechanisms that recognize and reward the contributions of others.

I want to take a moment to drive home the importance of showing gratitude in our personal relationships. With the people we live with, day in and day out, it can be easy to take them for granted and fail to acknowledge the value that they add in our lives. Many times, the longer our relationship lasts, the less we express gratitude to one another. We tend to assume that they know how we feel and therefore we don't need to tell them, or we simply get too busy or distracted to be intentional about expressing gratitude to our loved ones. Know this— there is a correlation between the health of a relationship and the amount of gratitude that is displayed toward one another. The more you incorporate gratitude and appreciation into your relationship, the healthier it will be. Conversely, if you do not choose to be intentional about thanking and appreciating your relationship partner, your relationship will grow unhealthy and potentially toxic.

Showing gratitude above the line means saying things like "thank you", and "I appreciate you", on a regular basis. It means telling those you love that you are thankful to have them in your life. It is being intentional about developing a gracious spirit concerning the relationship that you have with that person. Below the line gratitude looks like respecting the differences and boundaries of the other person. It means allowing those that you care about to know that you are thankful for them just the way they are. It is unconditional. Showing gratitude is not a conceptual thought, it is an action.

To sum it all up, how do we inspire those around us? Give to others. Serve those around you. Practice gratitude and appreciation. These are just a few of the things that you can begin doing to start inspiring those around you, no matter your level of charisma or eloquence. Inspiring others happens through the small choices you make every day to prioritize people and invest in relationships.

T- TIME

It's possible that one of the most critical elements to becoming a truly great leader is so simple that it is often overlooked—Time. While time management is incredibly important to any successful leader, it's not what I am referring to now. I believe that as a society we have traded the deep satisfactions and rewards that can only come with prolonged dedication, commitment and an investment of our time for the shallow assurances of instant gratification. Time is the great equalizer—we all have the same 24 hours in a day. The mark of a great leader can be seen in how they choose to invest their time not just occasionally, but over and over again. What do they choose to commit to and put their time towards every day? Going on a run once will leave you winded and out of breath, but running every day for a year will build stamina and condition your body to be ready for the race. The difference is not in how much time you put in on *one* day, it's how much *consistent* time you put in day after day over the course of a year.

The question is, how do great leaders choose to consistently use their time? While there is not one right answer to this question, there are two things that I have seen the most successful leaders I know investing time in consistently, and neither of them involve increasing productivity or working harder. In fact, the most successful leaders I know have consistently chosen to spend time over the course of their life investing in two types of relationships.

Time- Taking Time To Invest In Yourself

The most important relationship that you will ever have as a leader is your relationship with yourself. It is a rare leader who truly knows the importance of taking time to be alone and to spend time with themselves and on themselves. Some may call this investing in their own leadership, some may call it life-long learning, some may call it recharging or renewing, and some may call it self-care. Whatever you call it, it is critically important that you learn to take the time and find the stillness to listen to yourself and give yourself the time and resources that you need to be well and thrive.

Taking time for yourself has a great number of benefits, including the ability to sleep better, decreased fatigue and increased energy, a lessening of depression and anxiety and higher immunity to disease, just to name a few. The professional benefits include better decision-making, less frustration, and clarity of thought. Who wouldn't want to see benefits like this in their own life and leadership? And yet, so often, the thing that gets pushed to the very bottom of our priority list day after day, week after week, and year after year, is time for ourselves. We believe that we are too busy to slow down, find stillness, and invest in our own needs and wants. We are afraid that if we prioritize time for ourselves, we'll be seen as selfish, or high maintenance. Maybe most poignantly, we fear that taking time to be with ourselves means that we will have to confront ourselves, and we may not like what we see. Perhaps our fear of being lonely is driving us to avoid ever being alone.

Joan Cook wrote an article in *The Hill* (July 2019) an online news magazine that addressed this topic. She says that it is important for us to understand the differences between loneliness and aloneness. She reports that in our minds, we associate being alone with the negative effects of chronic loneliness such as: depression, alcoholism, drug abuse, suicidal thoughts and attempts, as well as early mortality. However, we misunderstand the difference in aloneness and loneliness, and in fact the exact opposite is true; aloneness is a key component to our mental and physical health. Cook says:

> When we are around other people, no matter how close we are to them, there are expectations of politeness and pressures to be favorable. And time spent with others can be taxing. Everyone needs time off stage, and escape from the roles we are expected to play, a release from our public persona, away from scrutiny and demand.

Cook reports that according to the recent research of Ester Schaler Bucchloz, it is a lack of solitude, and not an over-abundance of it, that contributes to many health dependencies and disorders. Cook concludes:

For sure, there are cultural differences in which solitude is accepted or promoted. But, for those who are part of this individualist world which pretty much dominates American mainstream culture, we require time alone. While alone time may naturally occur, at other times, we may need to create it.

Of course, each of us has to determine the optimal daily amount of alone time required for our good functioning. Be kind to your lone self and see how alone time may help you feel rejuvenated and able to feel more connected and present when with others. May each of us find the right amount of space, whether brief moments or extended hours.

Generally, when leaders read something about the importance of taking time for themselves, they nod their heads in agreement but in their heart, they've already decided that stillness, self-care, and personal time will not happen for them. Taking time for yourself seems like a good idea but we are rarely able to find the, well, time for it. We tend to view taking time for ourselves as a luxury that no one who wants to succeed in the "real world" can have. It sounds good and may be possible one day after we retire, we'll be able to do more of it, but the reality is that we are too busy and there are just too many demands on us.

I want to challenge this thought process and make a case for taking care of you. The greatest reason to take time for ourselves is that we cannot lead others past where we are willing to lead ourselves. If we are not going to grow our leadership, how we lead and influence others will be greatly affected. I believe that the real reason we did not take time to invest in ourselves is that we have not created the below the line discipline for this important leadership component.

Time - Taking Time To Invest In Others

The other kind of relationship that the most successful leaders invest in is their relationships with people closest to them—their spouses, children, families, and very closest friends. It's worth noting that it is relationships with those who are most important to them personally, and not professionally, that truly great leaders spend the most time to grow. Investing in our intimate personal relationships is maybe the most important thing we can do to further our professional success and certainly to ensure our personal satisfaction and happiness. The concept of "investing in personal relationships" may sound vague to you, so I'd like to offer one tactical skill that you can develop in order to improve every relationship in your life—listening.

Listening is a lost art in today's fast-paced society, where things move so quickly that we often overlook the chance to tune-in to the most important metric of how we're doing as leaders—the voices of those around us. Truly listening to understand takes time. It's not something that you do once a year or even once a quarter, but every single day. How we choose to be intentional about listening to others will look different from situation to situation and relationship to relationship, but if you want to truly lead those around you well, then you will find time and stillness to listen to them.

You may have noticed, as I have, that many times when we say we are listening, we're actually not. Someone else may be talking, and we may silent, but instead of listening to what they're saying and trying to understand their meaning and intention, we're busy formulating our response, or we are even totally checked out and thinking about an entirely different topic. Finding the time and having the skills to effectively listen may be one of the most difficult tasks for any leader. Listening is an active behavior that requires discipline and focus, but it certainly has huge benefits. When others are aware that you authentically want to hear what they are saying, their level of respect for you soars. People want to be heard more than they want to be agreed with, and they can only be heard when you endeavor to truly learn to listen.

I had a friend who recently went to the doctor. After a long wait, his physician quickly came into the room. My friend had what to him was an important issue to discuss with the doctor. However, the doctor made it clear that he did not have time to listen to my friend's story.

He instead directed my friend to tell his assistant about the issues. The physician was abrupt and rude. My friend left that appointment having lost respect for the doctor and vowing to find another physician who had the time and ability to listen to him. No one wants to entrust their health to someone who is unwilling to listen to their concerns. Neither does anyone want to give their time, energy, and effort to a boss or coworker who is unwilling to listen to them, and certainly no one wants to give their devotion and love to a partner who doesn't make them feel heard.

Listen to others and let them tell you what they need and how they need you to show up. It requires an investment of time and a dedication to creating stillness for others to be heard, but it might just be the thing that truly takes your leadership to the next level.

A Leader With GRIT

Allow me to introduce you to a friend of mine. His name is Captain Mike Coats. Mike is a war hero, although he would not be comfortable with that description. Mike graduated from the US Naval Academy and was assigned to the aircraft carrier USS Kitty Hawk. He flew 315 combat missions in Southeast Asia. He served as a flight instructor and a test pilot. He logged over 5000 hours flying time in 28 different types of aircraft and 400 carrier landings.

He has been awarded numerous honors, including the Defense Superior Service Medal, 3 Navy Distinguished Flying Crosses, 32 Strike Flight Air Metals, 3 Individual Action Air Medals, 9 Navy Commendation Medals with Combat "V", and the NASA Space Flight Medal. Mike was selected as a candidate and became a NASA astronaut. He is a veteran of three space shuttle flights and served as acting Chief of the Astronaut Office. Coats left the Astronaut corps and became an executive in the private sector. Eventually he was named Vice President of Advanced Space Transportation for Lockheed Martin Space Systems Company. He then was hired as the 10th director of the Johnson Space Center.

Mike Coats has experienced incredible highs and some very difficult days as well. Only those who served understand the volatility, danger and risks that go along with defending our country in times of war. Mike is one of those individuals. He was there when the Challenger shuttle exploded. He walked with the families of his friends who were killed in the explosion. When the shooting occurred at Columbine High School, Mike was living near the school and working as an executive at Lockheed Martin. Mike served the families in his community through that horrific time of tragedy. He was the Director at Johnson Space Center during a suicide murder on their campus. Once again, he walked with families through a time of extreme loss, hurt and grief.

Mike has had many incredible and unique experiences in life. He is a leader who has accomplished great things and without question earned the respect of many. However, all of the things that you have read about Mike Coats do not, in my opinion, represent his greatest leadership feat.

Allow me to tell you the rest of the story. Professionally, Mike is a celebrated hero and well-respected figure in his field. Personally, Mike recently celebrated his 50th wedding anniversary with the love of his life. However, Mike didn't take his bride to a romantic getaway to mark the occasion. He did not take her to an extravagant restaurant to celebrate 50 years of marriage. Instead, he did what he has done every day for many years now—he brought his wife a McDonald's milkshake.

His precious wife suffers from the terrible disease Alzheimer's. She currently resides in a memory care facility near their home. Every day Mike goes to the nursing home in the morning to make sure that his wife eats a good meal. He says that her disease has caused her to lose her appetite and he worries about her getting the appropriate amount of nutrition. Once he takes care of his wife in the morning, he goes about his chores for the day. In the evening he makes his ritual trip to McDonald's to get his wife a chocolate milkshake. "She loves chocolate shakes," he tells me. The staff at McDonald's know him by name and many times will begin making the shake when they see him in the drive through. He then takes the shake to his wife and sits with her for a while. Sometimes she knows him, sometimes she doesn't. Regardless, he shows up, day after day, chocolate shake in hand, to love her.

Mike's humility allows him to get over himself and forget all of his honors and accolades and choose instead to focus on serving his wife in the twilight season of her life. He faces this difficult and debilitating storm with courage. He is not afraid of the hard thing —he runs to it each day. He inspires his precious bride with the gift of a milkshake. He takes the time to be present and to listen to her every single evening. He receives and expects nothing in return.

There is no better example of a leader with GRIT. This is leadership at its finest.

CONCLUSION

Summary

Let's turn the corner and head toward the homestretch of Crossing the Line by taking a minute to look back on where we have been. We began with creating a foundation of understanding around what **above** and **below** the line means. We attempted to create clarity around leaders who are more comfortable on the people side of the line (above) and leaders who are more comfortable on the execution side of the line (below).

We then created specific ways that a leader above or below the line could be successful, leading out of his or her comfort zone. We learned the importance of Crossing The Line as leaders. Leading well above the line can be defined in this equation: E + P + C = FA which stands for: **Expectations + Priorities + Commitment = Focused Alignment**. We defined leading well below the line in the equation: G + D + A = ME which stands for: **Goals + Data + Accountability = Measured Execution**.

We then broke down the process to address each of the four personality traits above and below the line. We discussed what each personality characteristic needs to know in order to lead successfully from his or her personality quadrant. We also addressed what each personality needs to remember.

We took on the monster of fear that keeps us from leading above and below the line. We challenged ourselves to overcome fear by developing trust. You took a simple assessment to measure yourself trust and you took an assessment that focused on your team's trust level.

In order to lead effectively, there has to be alignment within the culture. You learned the equation A + B = C which stands for: **Actions + Belief = Culture**. We then challenged you to go above the line and answer the following questions: What is our purpose? What value do we provide? What are our habits? What does success look like? What are our priorities?

Next, we provided four tips to help you leap from individual competency to organizational capacity. These tips were:

1. Build up your relationships.
2. Don't do the work, enable the work.
3. Don't have all of the facts but stay engaged.
4. Get past the details and see the big picture.

We then processed the importance of IQ versus EQ. We challenged you to be someone who leads above and below the line with GRIT which stands for:

- **G**et over yourself.
- **R**un to the hard thing.
- **I**nspire others.
- **T**ake time.

You were challenged to apply these ideas and concepts not to just your professional life but your personal relationships as well. The reason that personal application is included in this book is because of a fundamental leadership truth; a good leader leads well at work and at home. Loving and serving those well who are in your personal life is the most important task that you can accomplish. Get that right, and the professional leadership skills will follow.

Our children are grown now, but when they were young and still in school, we made a commitment that I would greatly limit my travel. My wife and I knew the importance of being present in our children's lives as much as possible. That decision allowed me to coach basketball teams, participate in birthday parties, and attend play productions. It allowed me to be there for the homework woes and test grade celebrations. I have precious memories and not one regret about giving up some of my professional opportunities. I made a lot of mistakes as a parent, but this is one thing I believe I got right. Leading at home is where it all begins.

The Beach

I love the beach. In fact, as I'm writing this book, I am at the beach watching the waves splash against the beautiful white shores of Gulf Shores, Alabama. Perhaps that is why its easy for me to think of leadership much like the waves in the ocean. The waves continue to roll from day to day with extreme variations in their ripples toward the shore. Some days the waves are high, rough and threatening. Other days they are calm and gently approach the shore. Many days they are somewhere between those two extremes.

There are days when leading can be difficult, the stress level is high, and the expectations are rough and threatening. It is not always easy or fun to ride the waves of disruption and miscommunication. The roaring tides of transitions are rarely easy and almost always threaten a part of the team or organization.

Then there are the days that are calm. The stress level is down, and the demands are being met with excellence. The processes and systems provide a gentle flow of confidence and assurance that the tasks are being completed. This season of leading is fun and rewarding.

Like the waves in the ocean there is one thing that strong effective leaders will never do. They will never become stagnant. They must always be learning and growing no matter the size or difficultly of the waters. It is true that it is easier to think about learning during the seasons of calm. However, we learn more from our difficult days than our calm ones.

The waves of the ocean are never ever stagnant. Likewise, we as leaders can never allow ourselves to become stagnant and irrelevant if we want to continue to lead others well.

A Word About 2020

I began writing this book at the very end of 2019, before the coronavirus pandemic, and before the massive civil unrest took place in our country. In fact, we are living the consequences of both of these events now, as I write the conclusion to this book in August of 2020. It has never been more important for leaders to cross the line with focused alignment and measured execution.

The unique challenges of living through a global health crisis are compelling us to lead in a different way. Those who were able to cross the line with innovation and adaptability are succeeding. Those who held on to the thought processes of the past are struggling and may soon become irrelevant. Creating new expectations and priorities have become essential. Those who were committed to these concepts are experiencing focused alignment in our new normal. Businesses are expecting employees to stay home and be productive instead of coming to a brick-and-mortar building. Developing engagement around virtual meetings and creating work outcomes remotely must take priority. Those who are committed to these expectations and priorities are the teams, companies and organizations who are marching forward with focused alignment into the uncertain times that 2020 has delivered.

Likewise, setting goals, gathering data and ensuring accountability have taken on new dimensions during these new and strange days. Strong teams have committed to meet more often virtually to ensure engagement and clarity of goals. They work hard to find innovative new ways to track and deliver data that may be changing more rapidly than in the past. Accountability must occur without direct supervision in many cases. Therefore, the data and results must support and drive the accountability of a team. Successful teams are creating a rhythm of virtual meetings, data reporting and accountability of outcomes. They are learning a new way to proceed with measured execution. Crossing the line as a leader allows you to keep your team engaged and focused while executing by hitting the data driven goals.

This is the most important part of this book. We have recently experienced a tragic murder of George Floyd, and his death has brought about an awakening to the senseless deaths of other black men and women in our country. This, in my opinion, is the result of a long history of racism. I am a white male and therefore I cannot know the pain and frustration that the African American community has experienced because of systemic racism. I do know that my friends have suffered, black and white alike, and this causes me pain. I also know that we must address this issue in our country. It is my hope that this season in the life of our country will be one of authentically listening to one another and truly taking the time to hear and to understand. I hope that we can come together with men and women who expect to address this evil, that we set ending racism as a priority and we commit to leading change. We must be focused and aligned. We must set attainable goals for continued communication and action steps that will lead us toward our commitment. We need to keep gathering data and statistics so that we can hold ourselves and others accountable for making progress. We must have accurate measured execution if we hope to succeed in eradicating racism.

I am a follower of Jesus. Because He is my compass, I can in no way accept the degrading or demeaning of another human life. No matter who or what you use as your guiding compass, I challenge you to search your heart about racism. As leaders we must choose to lead this effort to offer respect and validation to those who have been hurt by the injustice of our society.

Thank you for taking the time to read this book. I hope it has challenged you both personally and professionally. Remember when you choose to Cross the Line as a leader, you will make a difference.

ACKNOWLEDGEMENTS

This book was written with the intent to offer a bit of insight and help with our personal and professional relationships. It was not, however, written alone. I used my superpower gift of pulling incredible people around me to accomplish this long and sometimes arduous project.

First, there is one person who instinctively knows my heart and voice. She committed to walk with me on this project. She challenged my thought process and spent countless hours improving the content and flow of this book. She is one of those gifted individuals who has the ability to produce excellence in anything she tackles. Her name is Lauren Little, and she is my daughter. Thank you, LP, I will be forever thankful for and proud of you. This book is significantly better because of your hard work and your commitment to not settle for average.

Once the content was written, the tedious task of editing was required. My extremely competent Camel wife, Melanie, was the perfect fit for the job. Thank you, Sweetie, for your sharp detailed eye. Finding and correcting all of my grammatical and other type of errors was a monumental task. Because of you, this work will read with many less typos and incorrect sentence structures. You are the quality of not just this book but of our relationship. I can't wait for our next travel adventure and I promise you, there will be no editing asked of you!

This book would be mere fiction or hypothesis if it were not for my friends who allowed me to walk with them and thus gain real life experiences. To those with whom I have the privilege of serving as your Executive Coach, thank you. You teach me and make me a better leader.

Melissa Jackson, my partner, and the team at Eagle Consulting are a constant source of encouragement and inspiration to me. Thank you for your leadership, friendship and belief in our vision to make a difference in the lives of others.

Finally, and most importantly, if there is anything good that is found in this writing it is because of the One named Jesus, who calls us to love another.

www.ingramcontent.com/pod-product-compliance
Lightning Source LLC
Chambersburg PA
CBHW021439210526
45463CB00002B/573